Chaffers'
Concise Marks & Monograms

Chaffers'

CONCISE MARKS & MONOGRAMS

on pottery & porcelain

William Chaffers

revised and augmented by Frederick Litchfield

Wordsworth Editions

First published as *The Collector's Handbook of Marks and Monograms on Pottery and Porcelain* by Reeves and Turner, London, 1908.

This edition published 1988 by Wordsworth Editions Ltd,
8b East Street, Ware, Hertfordshire.

Reprinted 1989
Reprinted 1990

ISBN 1-85326-915-8

Printed and bound in Great Britain by
Mackays of Chatham PLC, Chatham, Kent

EDITOR'S PREFACE

TO THE NEW EDITION

THIS New Edition of Chaffers' Hand-book is now published in a more complete form than the previous issues, and should be of greater service to the collector, for, in addition to some 500 marks which have been contributed by the Editor, there are a great many which the late Mr. Chaffers had inserted in his Seventh Edition of the large book, but which had not been included in his previous edition of the Hand-book. The present edition is, therefore, a complete excerpt or *résumé* as regards the marks of the original work, entitled "MARKS AND MONOGRAMS ON POTTERY AND PORCELAIN," by W. Chaffers, the last edition of which was revised by the present Editor.

No material change has been made in the arrangement of the work, which follows that of the larger book referred to above. The size is handy for the collector's pocket; and to maintain this desirable end, some of the larger marks have been reduced in scale and a lighter paper used, so as not to materially increase the bulk.

The following very slight historical outline sketch has been added by the Editor, which it is hoped will be of service to the collector.

The subject of the references in the following pages may be roughly divided into two classes—Pottery and

Porcelain. Pottery includes stoneware and enamelled or glazed earthenware; porcelain, that more vitreous and transparent composition of china clay and *petuntse* or ground flint, which is more akin to glass.

For the purposes of this Hand-book it is unnecessary to explain in further detail the differences in composition and texture of the two classes of Ceramics, but speaking generally, pottery breaks with a rough surface of its fractured parts, as would an ordinary piece of terra-cotta, while porcelain breaks with smooth surfaces, similar to glass.

To the Pottery class belong all those *fabriques* of enamelled earthenware called MAIOLICA, FAYENCE, or DELFT, these being the Italian, French, and Dutch subdivisions respectively, although the terms have become intermixed, and casually applied to all classes of faience.

The most famous of the Italian maiolica, first made in the later part of the fifteenth century, under the personal patronage and encouragement of the dukes or petty sovereigns of the little states and duchies into which Italy was then divided, are those of Urbino, Gubbio, Castel Durante, Pesaro, Faenza, and Caffagiolo, with many others, the marks of which occupy the first fifty pages of the Hand-book. Of the individual artists who decorated the ware, none is so celebrated as Maestro Giorgio Andreoli, more commonly known as Maestro Giorgio, who worked at Gubbio. Several of the characteristic and diversified signatures of this famous artist are given for the collector's reference, but as genuine specimens of this master have been so thoroughly searched for, and absorbed into museums and well-known private collections, the unskilled collector should be very sceptical in accepting any majolica attributed to Giorgio without the most convincing proofs of its authenticity.

The numerous FAYENCES of France and Holland, and to a much smaller extent those of other countries, will be found represented by their *fabrique* marks, and by the signatures or initials and monograms of the potters and artists who worked in their respective ateliers; and perhaps a word of caution may here be given as to the numerous imitations of the best known of such fayences, such as those of Rouen, Moustiers, Marseilles, and Nevers, also those of Delft, which are made in large quantities in Paris, and sold in England and on the Continent to unwary collectors.

The stoneware of Germany, commonly called "Gris de Flandres," also much of the old Fulham ware of England, and the exceedingly scarce and valuable "Saint Porchaire" fayence of France, formerly known as Henri Deux ware, also the decorative fayence of Persia and Rhodes, of Spain, called Hispano-Moresco, have scarcely any distinguishing marks, but such as there are will be found to follow those of Italy, France, and Holland.

The marks of the pottery of Staffordshire which are given, were placed by Mr. Chaffers in the English section at the end of the book, preceding the English *Porcelain* marks, and I have not thought it prudent to transfer them, although they rightly belong to the first part of the book.

PORCELAIN was made in China at a very early date, we do not know how early, but some centuries before its introduction into Europe; and the curious marks and hieroglyphics used by Oriental potters are given at considerable length, followed by those of Japan in the second section of the Hand-book. These singular characters, which appear to the casual observer as very similar to each other, have generally some meaning which relates to the article itself or to the purpose for which it was intended. Sometimes a proverb or legend, such as "Deep like a treasury of gems," or "For the public use in the General's Hall," is used as a mark; while, more generally, the Oriental characters refer to the date or place of manufacture, such as "Made in the King-te period of the great Sung dynasty."

It is, however, only right to state, in referring to marks on Chinese pottery and porcelain, that as the Chinese potters themselves have repeated the earlier marks and dates upon specimens of much later periods than such marks signify, the collector must not place reliance upon the marks, except when they agree with the apparent date of the specimen, as judged upon its merits with regard to its form and decoration.

The introduction, or rather the mention of the manufacture of porcelain in Europe, dates from the first few years of the eighteenth century, and is generally attributed to a chemist named Böttger, at Meissen in Saxony. Some of the early marks impressed in the red-brown paste which is identified with his name will be found, and also the numerous marks of the different periods of the most celebrated porcelain factory of Saxony, generally called DRESDEN.

From Meissen the secret of porcelain-making spread to Vienna, to other parts of Germany, and subsequently to France and England, gradually superseding the glazed earthenware or faience upon which so much artistic care had been lavished.

The famous Sèvres factory has a history which can be divided into chapters representing different classes of manufacture, and the marks and monograms of the numerous artists who decorated this most delicate and valuable porcelain are given at considerable length, and will enable the collector to trace to the date of its manufacture and the name of the decorator or gilder many a specimen in his cabinet.

The group of English *fabriques*, commencing with the famous Bow works, then with Chelsea and Derby, afterwards amalgamated under Mr. Duesbury into the Chelsea-Derby factory, the famous Worcester factory started by Dr. Wall, the Bristol and Plymouth works, also the much sought after Welsh factories of Nantgarw and Swansea, with others of less importance, all followed the lead of the Meissen porcelain manufactory. The *fabrique* marks and many of the potters' marks will be found under their respective headings.

The marks and monograms of the ceramic *fabriques* of the Continent and of England form a fascinating object of collection, and the study of the origin or *raison d'être* of these various marks is in itself a most interesting and instructive hobby, carrying the collector into glimpses of international and family histories which will well repay his time and attention.

INDEX

OF

MANUFACTORIES, MANUFACTURERS AND ARTISTS,

WITH THEIR MARKS AND MONOGRAMS, ETC.

Marks and Monograms

ON

POTTERY & PORCELAIN

·1531·
·f· X. A. R:
·T Urbino.

F: co. X:
Rou:

·1539·
·X·

X

X· N

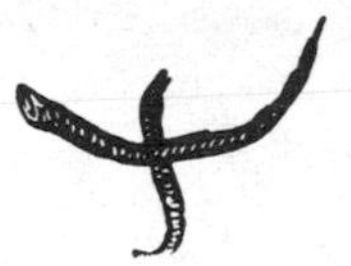

C
URBINO.

fran: Auello Roy:

1532
fra: Xanto. A. da
Rouigo, i. Vr
bino. pt:

URBINO. XVI Century.
Fra Xanto Avelli da Rovigo.

M·D·XXXIII·
·Fra Xato·A·
da Rouigo.
Urbino·

URBINO.

X
'1544,

X e Z
A

Q
Y
H

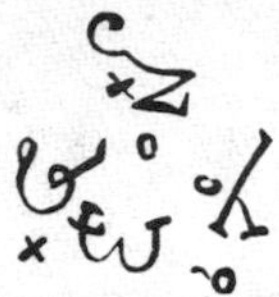

URBINO. XVI Century.
Characters found on Xanto's works.

Nicola da
·V·

Ihistoria de Sancta
Cicilia la qualle
e fata m botega de
guido da castello
durante
In VrBino 1528

URBINO.

da Vrbino

NICOLO DA URBINO.
XVI Century.

In botega di M°
Guido durã
tino
1532

Nella Botega
di Mº Guido
Durātino
In Urbino

URBINO. Guido Durantino.

nē 1551
fato in Botega
de guido merlino

URBINO. Guido Merlino.

fatte in Urbino
in Botega de
Mº Guido
fontana
Vasaro:

URBINO.

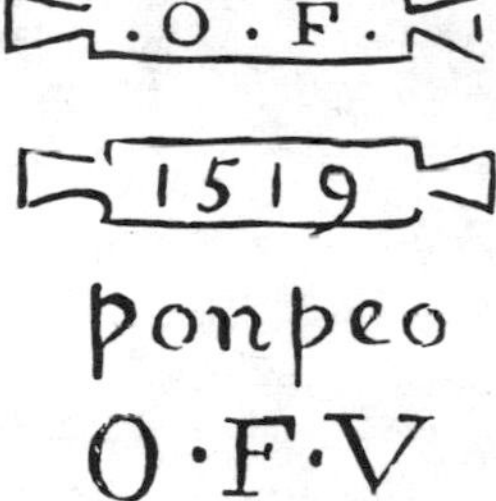

URBINO.

URBINO.

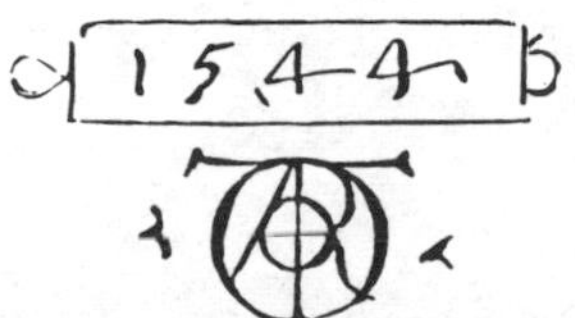

URBINO. XVI Century.
Marks attributed to Orazio Fontana.

URBINO. Flaminio Fontana.

· F · F ·

URBINO.

URBINO, 1542.

Gjone

URBINO. XVI Century.

Urbino—
L

URBINO. XVI Century.

Nel anno de le
tribulatio ni
d'Italia adi
26 de luglio
I Urbino

URBINO, 1536.

E.F.B.
1594

URBINO.

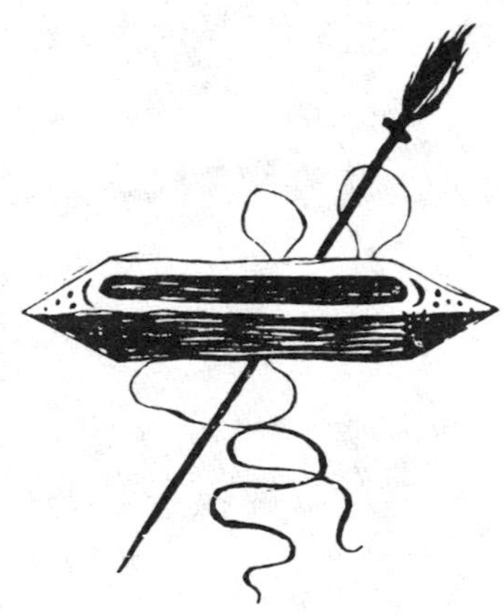

URBINO, 1523.

G · B · F ·

· 1630 ·
· G · B · F ·

URBINO.

In Urbino nella
botteg di Francesco
de Siluano
MDXXXXI

URBINO, 1541.

·ALF·P·F·
VRBINI
1606

URBINO. Alfonso Patanazzi.

ALFONSO PATANAZZI
FECIT
VRBINI 1606

Gironimo
urbin fecie
1583

URBINO.

A.P.

URBINO. Alfonso Patanazzi.

Vrbini Patana
fecit anno 1584

URBINO. Patanazzi.

F.P.
1617.

URBINO. Francesco Patanazzi.

1526

URBINO.

1534
Vrbinj

URBINO. Luca Cambiasi.

URBINO.

URBINO, 1531.

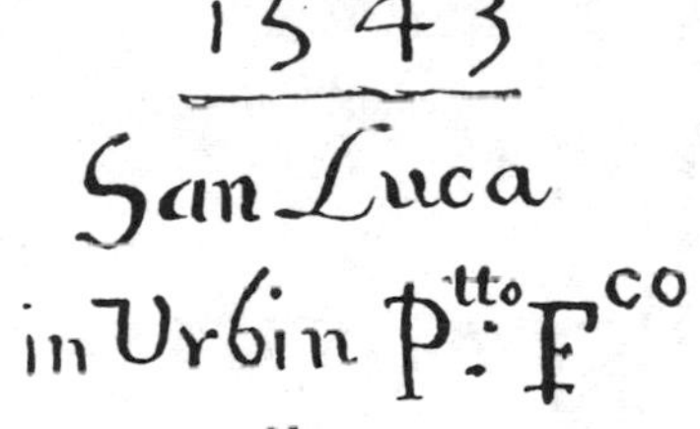

URBINO.

URBINO.

URBINO.

·f·L·R·

URBINO, 1529.

‹L.:.F›
1550

URBINO.

IUrbino-B

URBINO. XVI Century.

URBINO. XVI Century.

URBINO or FAENZA. Cesari Cari ?

Fabrica di Maiolica
fina di Monsiur Rolet
in Urbino. a 28 Aprile 1773

URBINO, 1773.

A

GUBBIO.

G

GUBBIO.

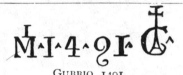

GUBBIO.
M°. Giorgio Andreoli, 1519–1537.

M·I·4·9·I·

GUBBIO, 1491.

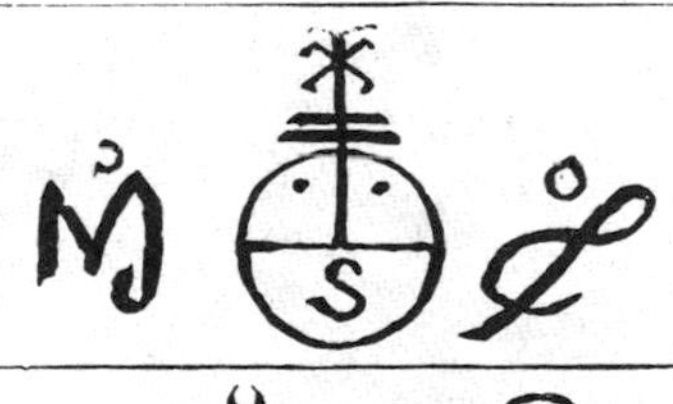

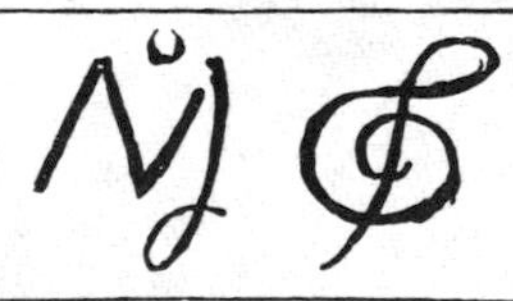

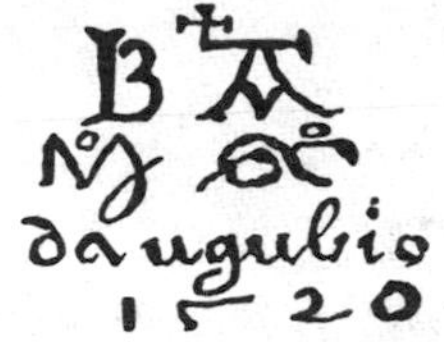

GUBBIO. Maestro Giorgio.

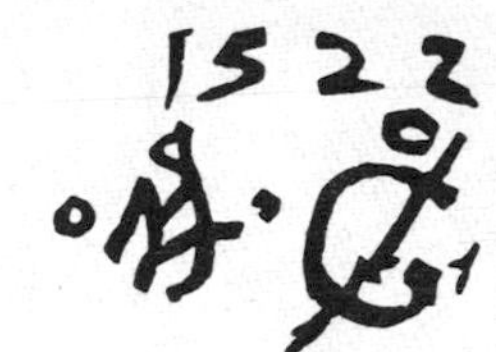

di 25 di
otobre
1519

GUBBIO.

15 25

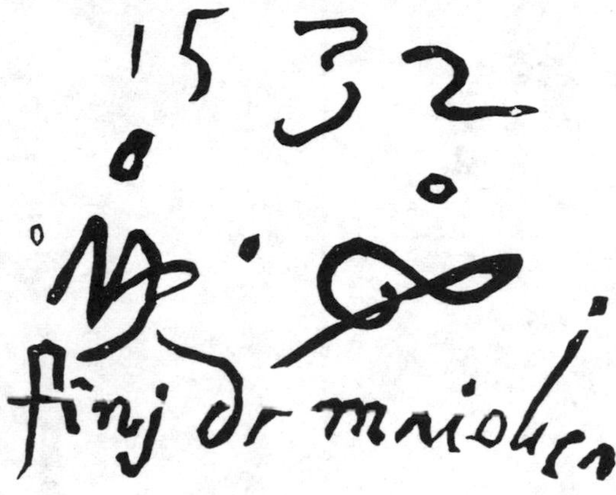

Matr: Gio:

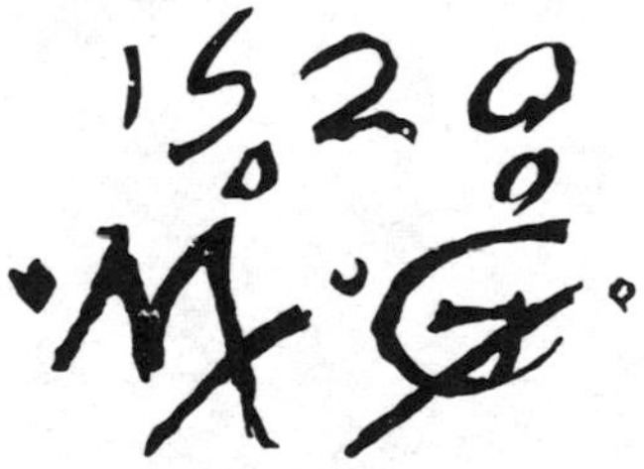

GUBBIO. Maestro Giorgio.

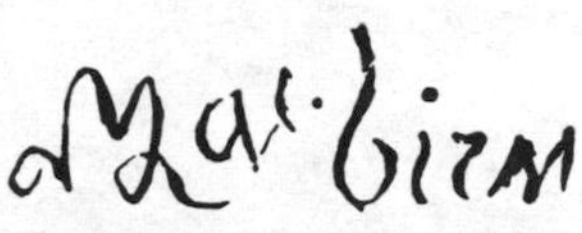

1537

GUBBIO. Maestro Giorgio.

GUBBIO. Maestro Giorgio, 1525.

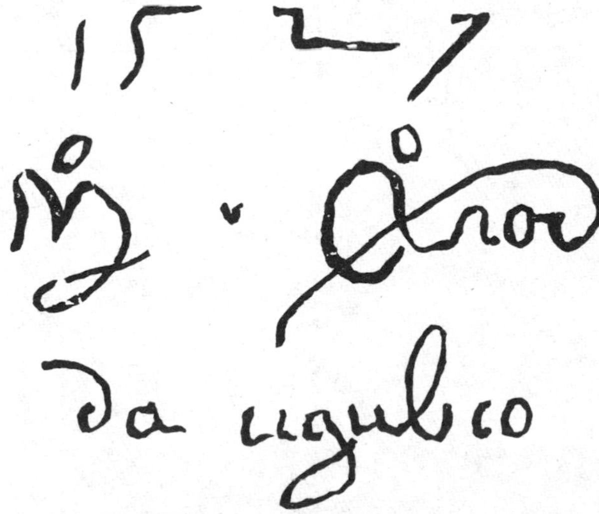

GUBBIO.

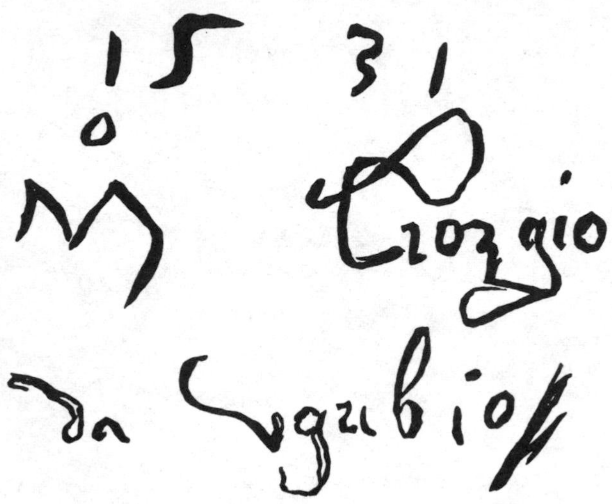

GUBBIO.

GUBBIO.

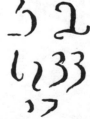

GUBBIO.

GUBBIO. Mº. Giorgio:

GUBBIO, 1518.

GUBBIO.

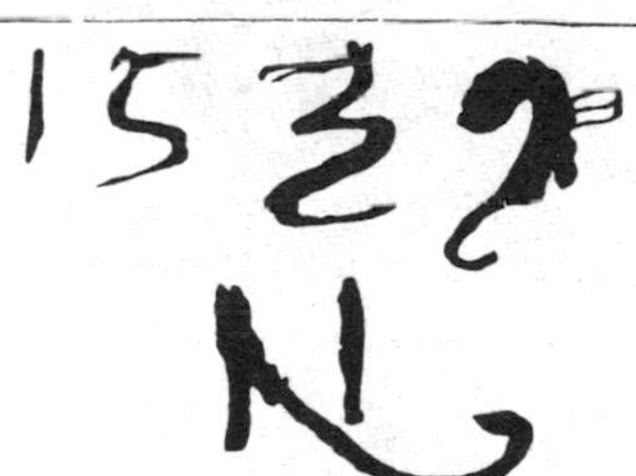

1535
N

GUBBIO, 1535.

P

GUBBIO. M°. Perestino.

1557
adi 28 de magio
in gûbio p mano
d maestro prestino

1533
.D.

GUBBIO. M°. Perestino.

C 1536
PERESTINO
1536

GUBBIO. M°. Perestino.

GUBBIO.

NG

GUBBIO.

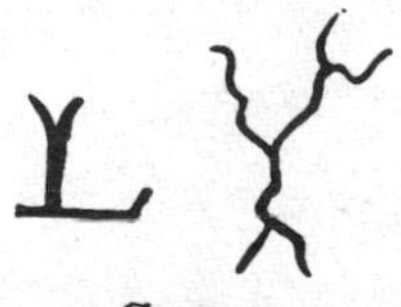

GUBBIO.

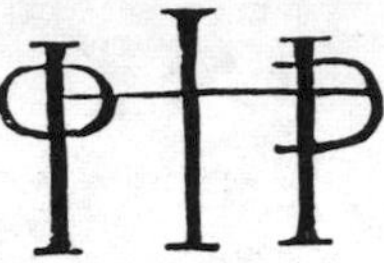

GUBBIO.

1541

GUBBIO.

GUBBIO.
M°. Salimbene. XVI Century.

GUBBIO.

GUBBIO.

GUBBIO, 1540.

·I·

GUBBIO. XVI Century.

M.A.I.M.

GUBBIO. XVI Century.

GABRIEL DA GUBBIO.

GUBBIO. XVI Century.

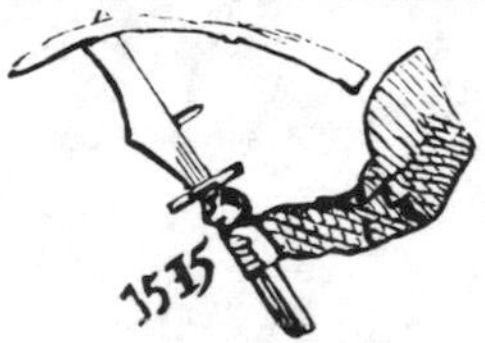

GUBBIO, 1515.

GUBBIO. XVI Century.

GUBBIO. XVI Century.

GUBBIO. M°. Cencio.

GUBBIO. Carocci, Fabri & Co. 1862.

fatto in pesaro 1542
in dottega di mᵒ gironimo
vasaro
iachomo pinsit

PESARO. Maestro Gironimo.

Cicerone et zulio Cesar
cuãdo idete le lege 1542
in la botega de mastro
girolame da legabice
In pesaro

PESARO, 1542.

1566
MVT. S C.E.
PISAVRI

PESARO, 1566.

O+A
1582

PESARO.

ell:r·P.C.P.1757.

PESARO?

Pesaro 1771.

C. I C
pesaro
1765
P. P. L.i:

PESARO.
Callegari & Cassali. Pietro Lei pinxit.

1508 adi 12 de setẽ
fata fu i Castel durãte
Zouã maria vro

CASTEL DURANTE.
Giovanni Maria Vasaro, 12th Sept. 1508.

CASTEL DURANTE. Sebastiano Marforio.

p mastro simono
in Castelo durāte

CASTEL DURANTE. M°. Simono. XVI Century.

1524
In Castel Du
rante

1526
jn castel
durante

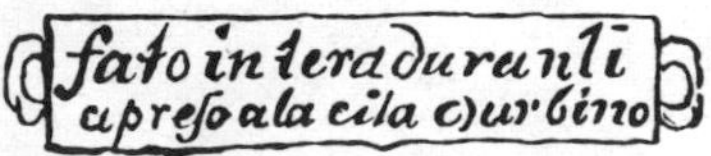

CASTEL DURANTE. XVI Century.

FRANCESCO DURANTINO VASARO. 1553.

CASTEL DURANTE.

CASTEL DURANTE.
M°. Pietro. XVI Century.

Hippollito Rombaldotti
Pinse in Urbania

CASTEL DURANTE. XVII Century.
Called Urbania, 1635.

frãcesco durantino
1544

CASTEL DURANTE.

CASTEL DURANTE.

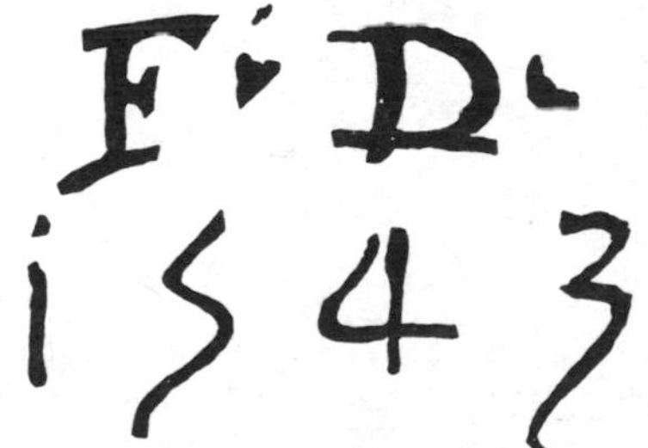

CASTEL DURANTE.

CASTEL DURANTE. XVI Century.

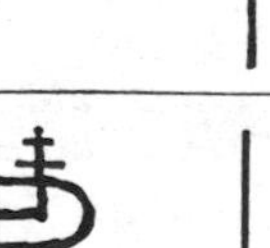

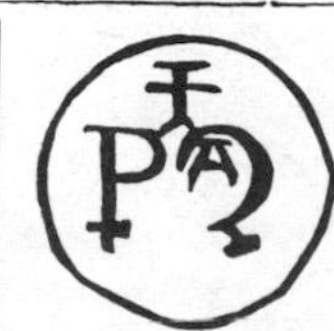

CASTEL DURANTE.
Merchants' marks. XVI Century.

CASTEL DURANTE.

GIOVANNI PERUZZI
DIPINSE, 1693.
CASTEL DURANTE.

CASTEL DURANTE.

Guidō saluaggio

CASTEL DURANTE.

S:R

CASTEL DURANTE.

Francesco Durātino
Vasaro Amōte Bagnole
et Perosscia 1553

PERUGIA.

NICOLAUS ORSINI
MIIII77
ADI 4 DI GENAIO

FAENZA. Nicolaus Orsini, 1477.

M I
ANDREA DI BONO PO

FAENZA. Andrea di Bono, 1491.

E O
AIG·YHTA

FAENZA. XVI Century.

F F F
F Z F

FAENZA. XVI Century.

NICOLAUS DE RAGNOLIS
AD HONOREM DE ET
SANCT MICHAELIS
FECIT FIERI FANO 1475

FAENZA. Nicolaus de Ragnolis, 1475.

FATO IN FAENZA
IN CAXA PIROTA

1525.

DON SIORSIO

Faenza. Don Giorgio, 1485.

IN FAENCA

XVI Century.

Faenza. XVI Century.

Faenza. XVI Century.

Faenza, 1525.

Faenza. XVI Century.

Faenza or Pesaro.

FAENZA or PESARO.

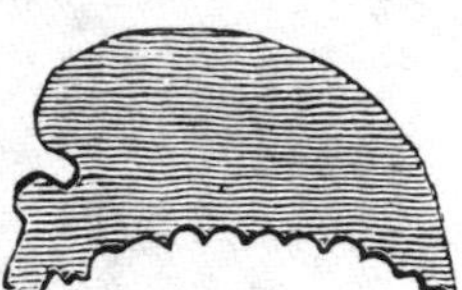

FAENZA. XVI Century.

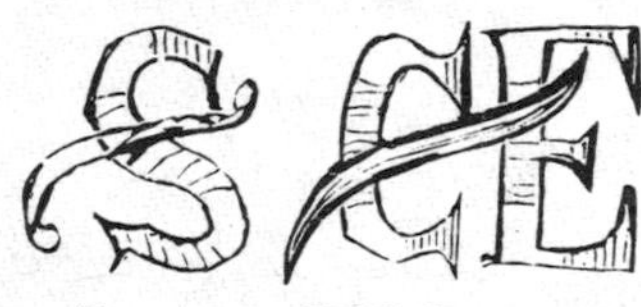

FAENZA. XVI Century.

FAENZA.

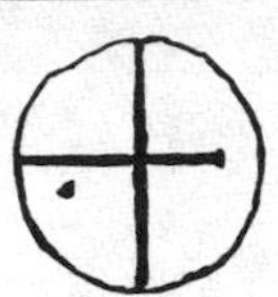

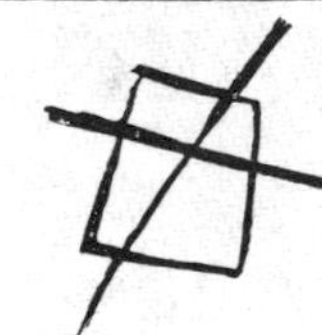

FAENZA.

FAENZA. XVI Century.

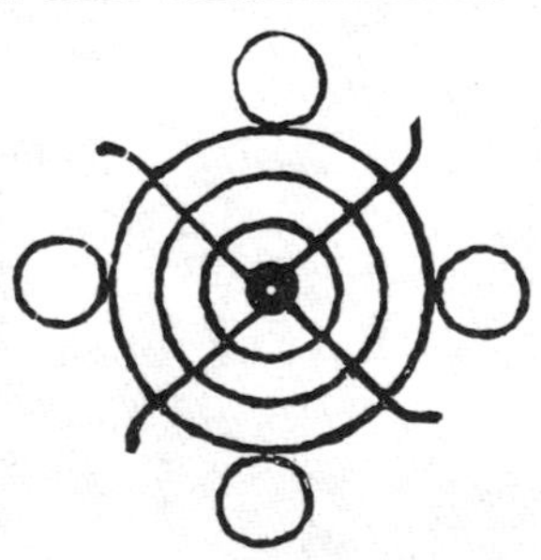

FAENZA.

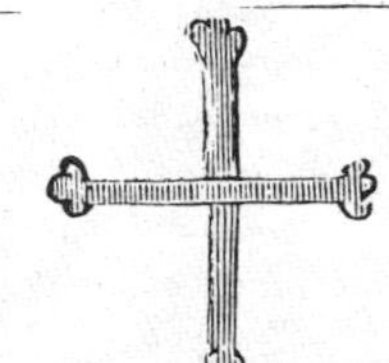

FAENZA. XVI Century.

MCCCCCXXXV

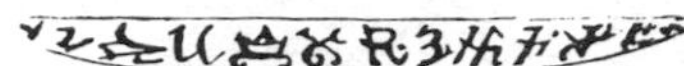

FAENZA, 1535.

FAENZA, 1520.

FAENZA. XVI Century.

FAENZA. XVI Century.

FAENZA.

FAENZA. XVI Century.

FAENZA. XVI Century.

FAENZA. XVI Century.

FAENZA, 1482.

MDXX
XIIII
F. ATNAN
ASIVS
B M

FAENZA 1534.

FAENZA. XVI Century.

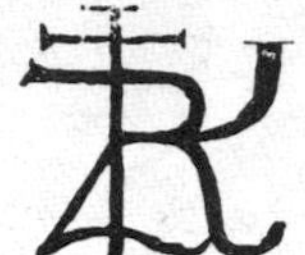

FAENZA. XVI Century.

Baldasara
manara

FAENZA. XVI Century.

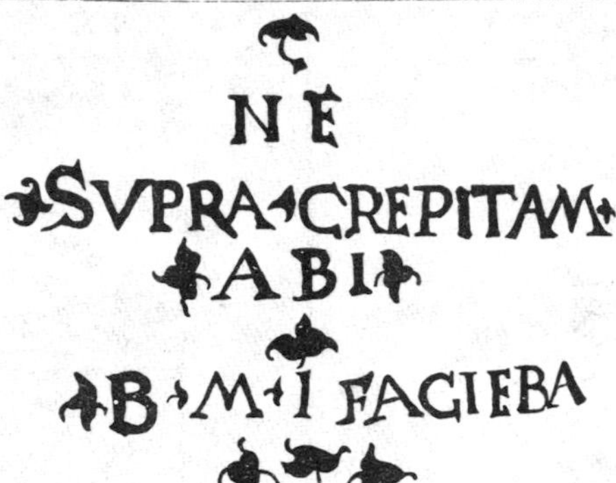

FAENZA.

MILLE CINQUE CENTO
TRENTASEI A DI TRI
DI LUIE
BALDASARA MANARA
FAENTIN FACIEBAT.

FAENZA, 1536.

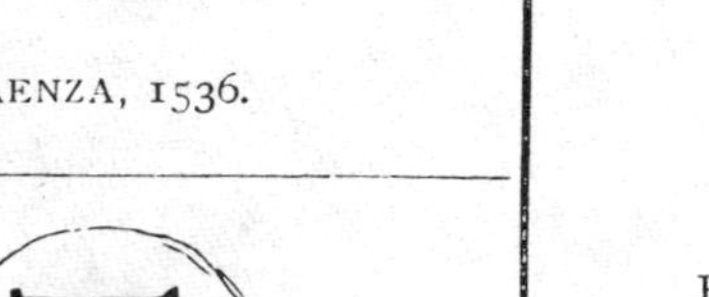

FAENZA. XVI Century.

FAENZA.

FAENZA. XVI Century.

FATO NELLA BOTEGA DI
MAESTRO VERGILLIO
DA FAENZA
NICOLO DA FANO.

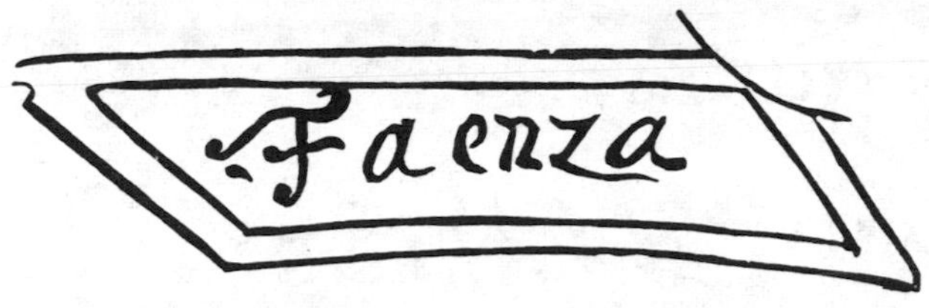

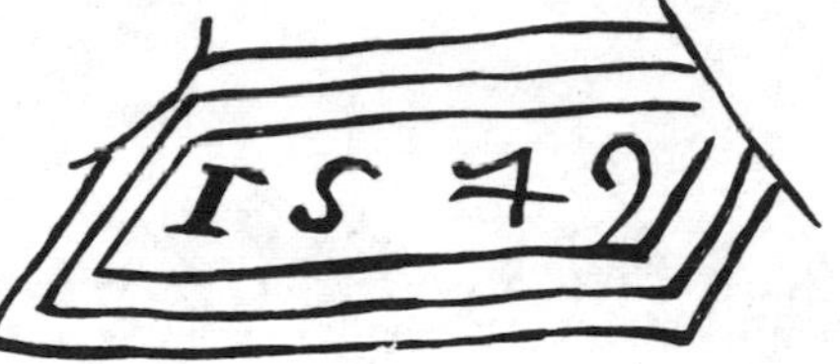

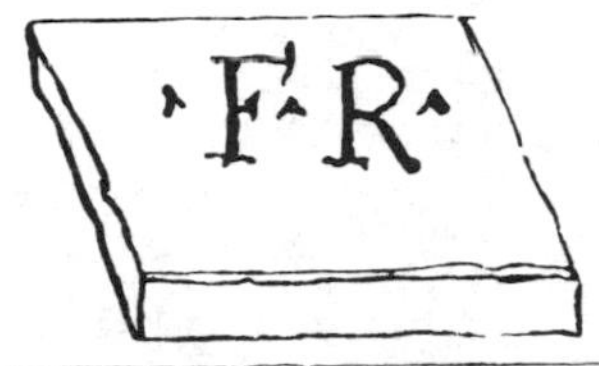

F R

FAENZA. XVI Century.

FAENZA. XVI Century.

FAENZA. XVI Century.

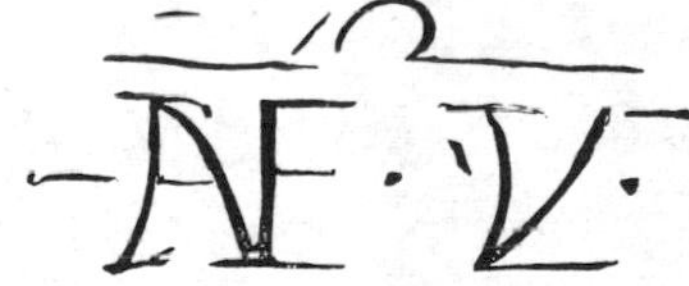

FAENZA or VENICE. XVI Century.

FAENZA, 1525.

FAENZA

FAENZA, 1546.

Fnnius raynerius F·F·1575

Gio: BAPTISTA·R·L

FAENZA. Rainerius, 1575.

FAENZA.

MX·MX

FAENZA, 1548.

FAENZA.

1563
adi 15 zenavo
fiu giouani Batista
da faenza
In Verona

VERONA, 1563.

DIRUTA. XVI Century.

DIRUTA. XVI Century.

.1545.
in deruta
grate fecit

DIRUTA.

1537
franco Urbini.
i deruta

G.V

DIRUTA. XVI Century.

DIRUTA. XVI Century.

DIRUTA, 1544.

DIRUTA. XVI Century.

fatta in diruta

DIRUTA.

. T. Deruta
El frate pinsi

DIRUTA.

D
1539
G S

DIRUTA.

jnderuta
1554

LD
1579

DIRUTA.

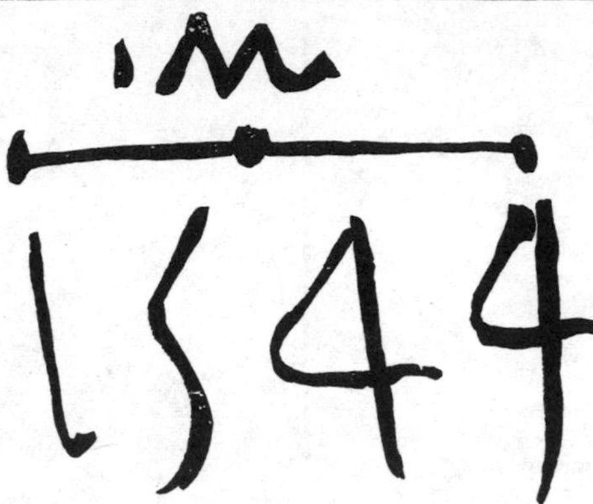

DIRUTA.

.IO·SILVEST.RO D'AGEI
OTRINCIDADERVTA:
FATTº IN BAGNIOREA
·I691

BAGNIOREA.

fabriano
1527

FABRIANO, 1527.

DIRUTA. XVI Century.

RIMINI. XVI Century.

Jn arimin·

RIMINI. XVI Century.

IN RIMINO
1535.

FATO IN
ARIMINENSIS
1635.

FORLI. XVI Century.

FORLI. XVI Century.

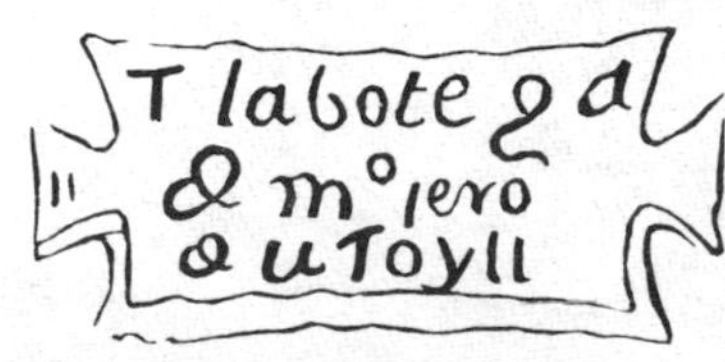

FORLI. XVI Century.

FORLI. XVI Century.

RAVENA. XVI Century.

FORLI, 1513.

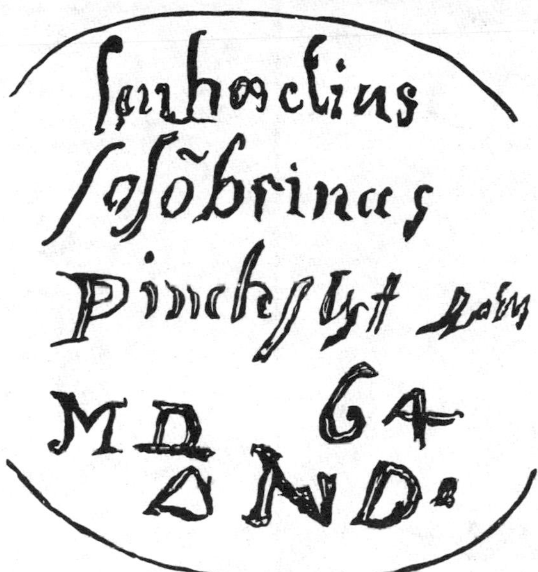

FORLI. Leuchadius Solombrinus, 1564.

RAVENA.

VITERBO. 1544.

IN CHAFAGGIOLO
FATO ADJ 21 DI JUNIO
1590.

TREVISO, 1538.

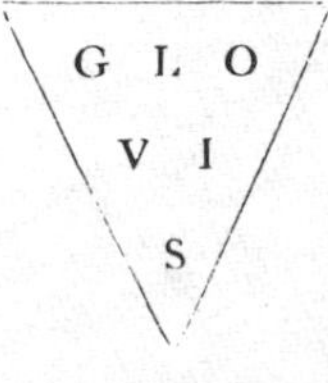

CAFFAGIOLO.

CAFFAGIOLO. XVI Century.

CAFFAGIOLO. XVI Century.

CAFFAGIOLO, 1531.

CAFFAGIOLO. XVI Century.

CAFFAGIOLO.

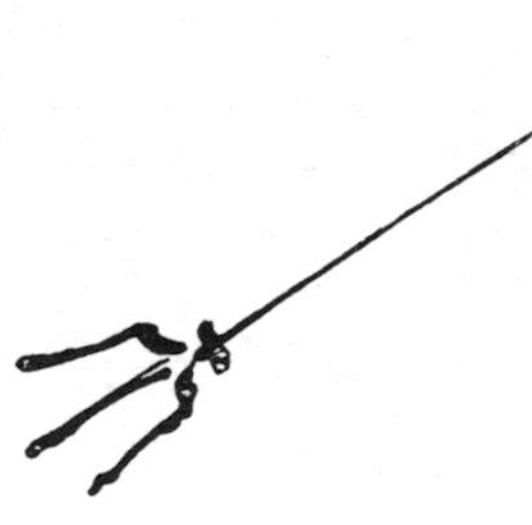

CAFFAGIOLO.

CAFFAGIOLO. XVI Century.

CAFFAGIOLO. XVI Century.

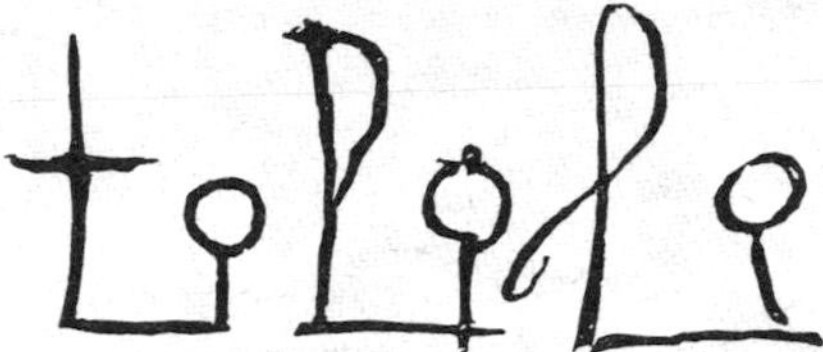

CAFFAGIOLO.

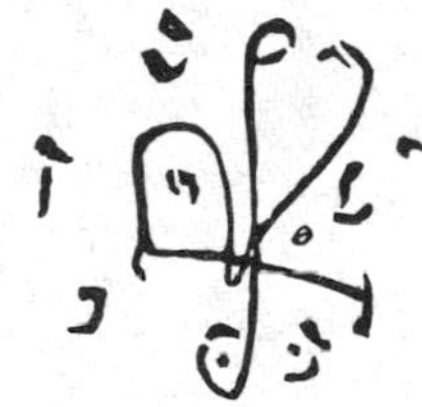

CAFFAGIOLO.

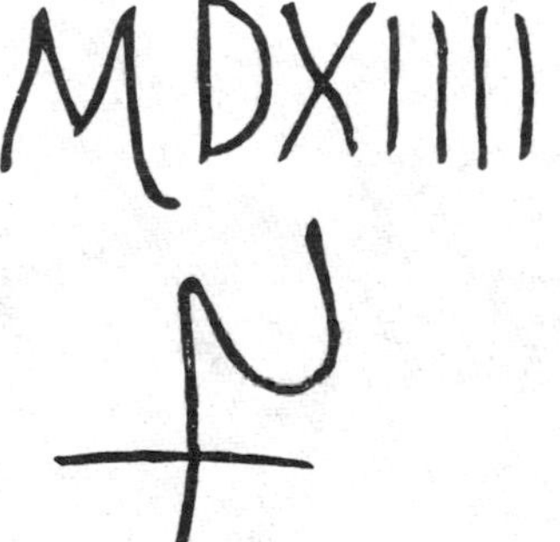

CAFFAGIOLO, 1514.

CAFFAGIOLO. XVI Century.

CAFFAGIOLO. XVI Century.

CAFFAGIOLO. XVI Century.

CAFFAGIOLO.

IN GAFAGIZOTTO.

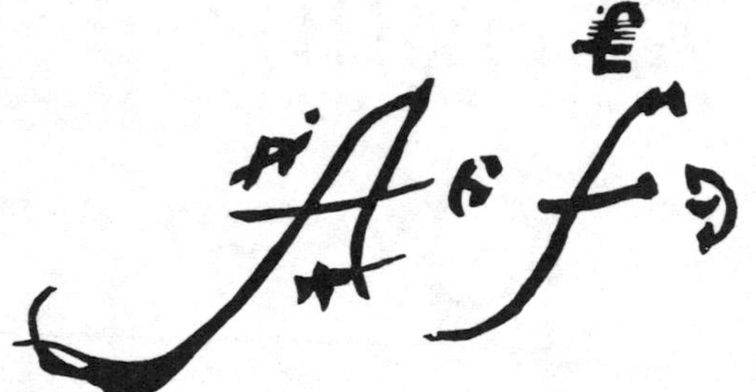

CAFFAGIOLO (In. Galiano), 1547.

G

FECE·GIOVANNI·ACOLE

1509

CAFFAGIOLO, 1509.

CAFFAGIOLO.

CAFFAGIOLO, 1507.

CAFFAGIOLO.

CAFFAGIOLO.

GEO:BATA:MERCATI
1649

BORGO S. SEPOLCHRO.

SAN QUIRICO. XVIII Century.

I.P.

SIENA, 1542.

SIENA, 1510–1520.

SIENA. XVI Century.

TERENZIO ROMANO
SIENA 1727.

BAR. THERESE ROMA.

SIENA. XVIII Century.

FRE. BERNARDINUS.
DE SIENA. IN. B. S. SATUS

TERCHI.

SIENA. XVIII Century.

Bar Turc
Romano.

SIENA. XVIII Century.

Ferdinando Maria Campani
Senese dipinse 1733

SIENA. F. M. Campani.

SIENA.
Ferdinando Campani. XVIII Cent.

F. C.

SIENA. XVIII Century.

BAR. TERCHI. ROMANO

SIENA. XVIII Century.

In Venetia in Cõtrada dj Sta Polo in
botega dj M^o^ Lodouico

VENICE. Circa 1530.

ZENER DOMENIGO
DA VENECIA
FECI IN LA BOTEGA
AL PONTESITO DEL
ANDAR A SAN POLO.
1568

VENICE, 1510.

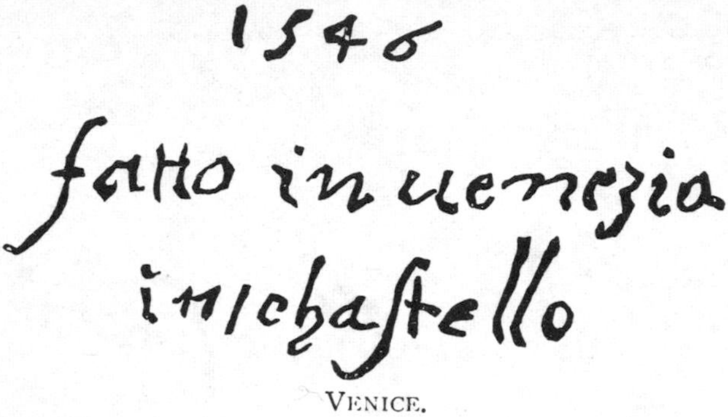

1546

fatto in uenezia

inchastello

VENICE.

Adi, 13, Aprille, 1543,

AOLASDINR

VENICE, 1543.

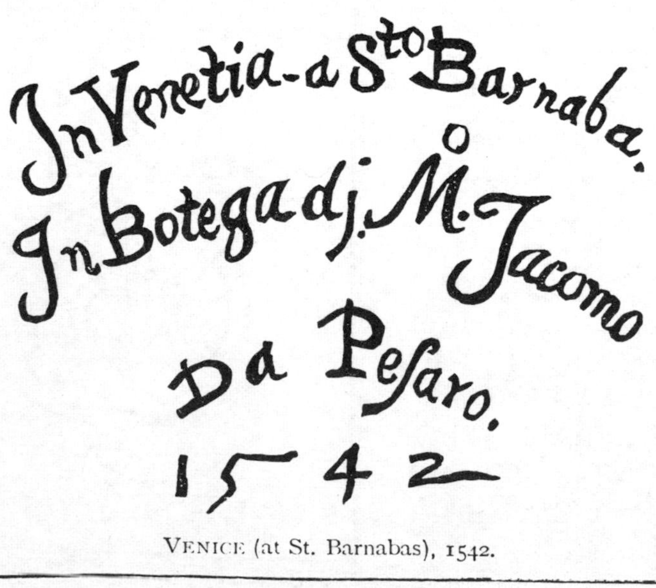

In Venetia-a S^to Barnaba.

In Botega dj. M^o. Jacomo

Da Pesaro.

1542

VENICE (at St. Barnabas), 1542.

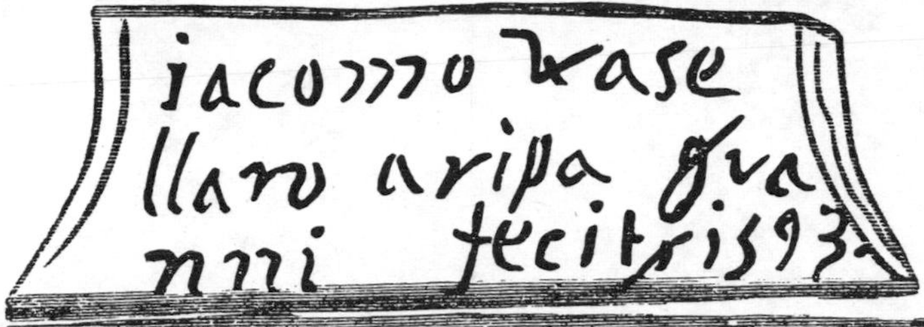

VENICE, 1593.

1622

Dionigi Marini

1636

VENICE.

Io Stefano Barcella

Veneziano Rox

VENICE. XVII Century.

VENICE.
Established 1753; ceased 1763.

VENICE. Circa 1760.

VENICE. Circa 1760.

VENICE. Circa 1760.

VENICE. Circa 1760.

Venice (Garofalo). Circa 1766.

VENICE. Circa 1700.

VENICE. XVIII Century.

VENICE. Circa 1750.

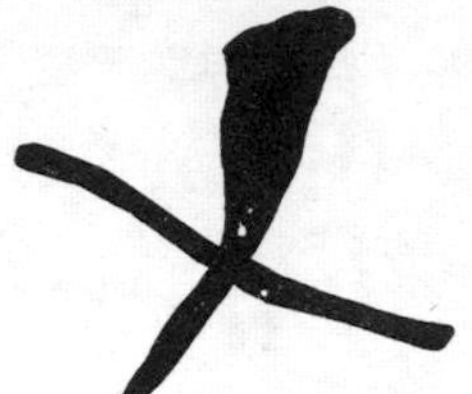

VENICE.

VENICE. XVIII Century.

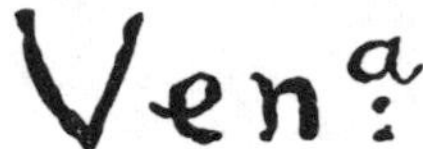

VENICE. XVIII Century.

VENICE. XVII Century.

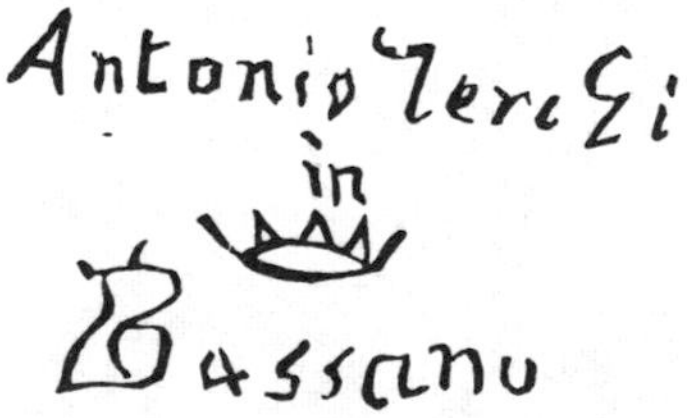

Antonio Terchi
in
Bassano

BASSANO. XVII Century.

B° Terchj
Bassano

BASSANO. XVII Century.

Della fabrica di
Gio Batt[a] Antonibon
nelle nove di Decen
1755.

NOVE.

ue
No:
G:B:A:B:

NOVE. Antonibon circa 1730.

Fab[a]. Baroni Nove.

NOVE. Circa 1805.

P: A: Crosa

CANDIANA. XVII Century.

BL. 1429
FACEBAT

FLORENCE.

LR = FA
1454

FLORENCE.
Attributed to Luca della Robbia.

X
1563
a padoa

PADUA. XVI Century.

F. F. F.I.

FLORENCE. XVII Century.

PADUA. XVI Century.

A. PADOA ✠
1564.

CASTELLI. XVIII Century.

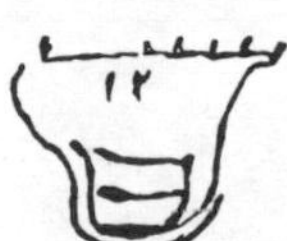

CASTELLI. XVIII Century.

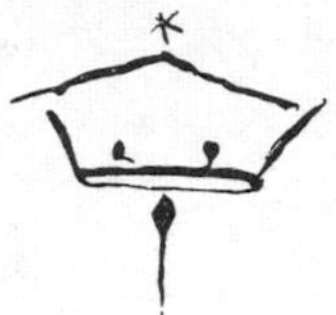

CASTELLI. XVIII Century.

iOĀNESGRVĀ FECIT

CASTELLI. XVIII Century.

Dr. Franc. Antº. Cavr. Grue P.

CASTELLI. Circa 1730.

Fr. A. Grue esepraì. 1677.

CASTELLI.

D.R Grue pinxit.

CASTELLI. Circa 1730.

CASTELLI.

S. Grue.

CASTELLI. Saverio Grue, circa 1780.

S. Grue P Napoli. 1749.

CASTELLI.

L G P.

CASTELLI. Liborius Grue, circa 1750.

L S Grue

CASTELLI. XVIII Century.

SG pt

CASTELLI. Saverio Grue, circa 1780.

S. G. P.

CASTELLI. Saverio Grue, 1780.

SG. P.

CASTELLI. Saverio Grue; died 1806.

CASTELLI. Circa 1750; died 1776.

Gentili P

CASTELLI. XVIII Century.

Math. Roselli fec.

CASTELLI.

Joannes-m.s: de düÿ ts·A:s .F. M·DL·LXII

CASTELLI.

G. Rocco di Castelli.

1732.

CASTELLI.

CASTELLI. Carlo Coccorese, 1734.

Lvc·Ant°. Ciañico P.
1733

CASTELLI.

NAPLES. XVII Century.

P.il Sig.ri Francha
I
Nepita
1682.

NAPLES.

HF

H. F.

NAPLES. XVII Century.

F.D.V

N.

NAPLES.
F. Del Vecchio. XVII Century.

Giustiniani

I N

NAPLES. XVIII Century.

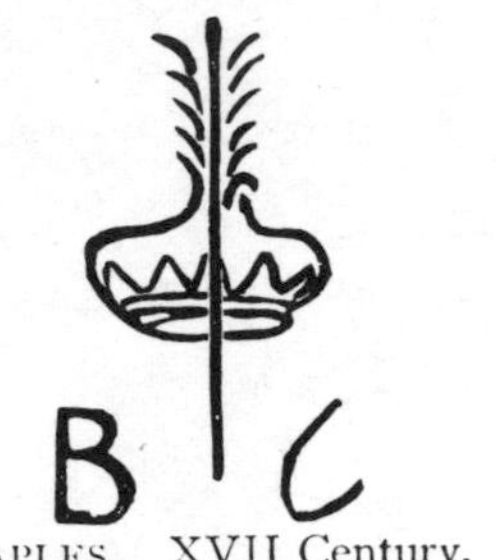

NAPLES. XVII Century.

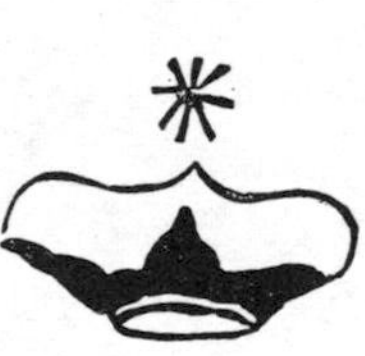

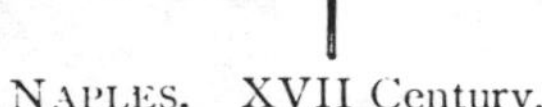

NAPLES. XVII Century.

NAPLES. XVIII Century.

NAPLES. XVIII Century.

NAPLES. XVIII Century.

F. & G. Colonnese
Naples.

XIX Century.

LODI.

LODI. XVIII Century.

LODI. XVIII Century.

RAFAELLO
GIROLAMO
FECIT
M^{TE} L^{PO}
1638

MONTELUPO.

Dipinta Giovinale
Tereni da Montelupo.

XVII Century.

MONTELUPO, 1663.

MONTELUPO. XVI Century.

MONTELUPO.

M
1627

MONTELUPO.

Milano

XVIII Century.

SI·FECE·QVESTO·PIATELO:
IN·BOTTECHA·DI·BECHONE
DEL·NANO·IN·SAMINIATELO
CHVESTO·TTAITO·AGHOSTINO
DI·MO.A.DI·CINQE·DI·
GVGNIO· 1581.

SAN MINIATELLO.

Milano
F 4 C

XVIII Century.

Mil

MILAN. XVIII Century.

F
Pasquale Rubati
Mil^o^.

MILAN. XVIII Century.

MILAN. XVIII Century.

Mre Trecchi

MILAN. XVIII Century.

MILAN. XVIII Century.

MILAN. XVIII Century.

Fatta in
Torino adi
12 d setēbre
1577

TURIN, 1577.

TURIN. XVII Century.

Fabrica
Reale di
Torino
1737

TURIN. XVIII Century.

GRATAPAGLIA
FE:TAVR·

TURIN. XVIII Century.

VINEUF. (Turin.)

TURIN.

TURIN.

TURIN. XVIII Century.

Laforest en
Savoye
1752.

TURIN.

Thomaz Masselli
Ferrarien fec

FERRARA. XVIII Century.

GENOA. XVIII Century.

GENOA. XVIII Century.

GENOA. XVIII Century.

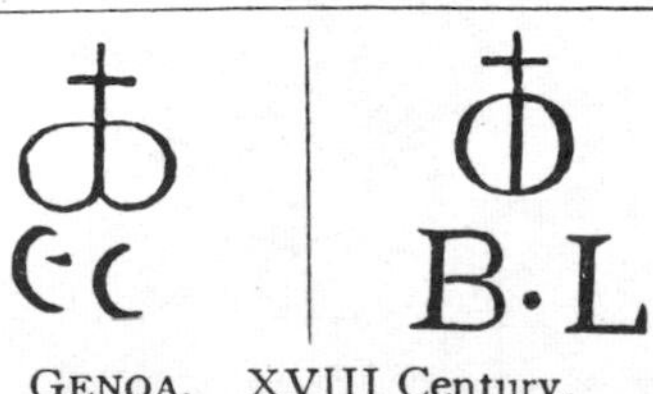

GENOA. XVIII Century.

GENOA. XVIII Century.

GENOA. XVIII Century.

SAVONA. XVIII Century.

SAVONA. XVIII Century.

S.A.G.S.

SAVONA. XVIII Century.

SAVONA. XVIII Century.

AGOSTINO RATTI
SAVONA. 1720.

SAVONA.

B ◇ C
1743

SAVONA. XVIII Century.

SAVONA. XVIII Century.

SAVONA. XVIII Century.

SAVONA. XVIII Century.

SAVONA. XVIII Century.

SAVONA. XVIII Century.

SAVONA. XVIII Century.

SAVONA. XVIII Century.

SAVONA. XVIII Century.

SAVONA. XVIII Century.

SAVONA. XVIII Century.

SAVONA. XVIII Century.

SAVONA. XVIII Century.

SAVONA. XVIII Century.

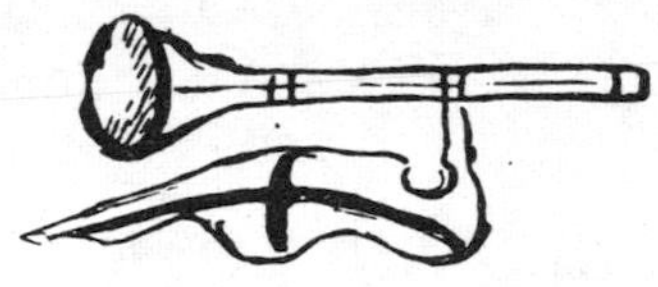

SAVONA. XVIII Century.

Jacques Borrelly, Savonne,
1779, 24 *Septembre.*

ESTE
G.

ESTE. XVIII Century.

jacques Boselli

SAVONA.

PRESBYTER ANTONIUS
MARIA CUTIUS PAPIENSIS
PROTHONOTARIUS
APOSTOLICVS FECIT
ANNO DOMINICÆ 1695.
PAPIÆ 1695.

PAVIA.

MB orrelli Inuent
Pinx: A:S 1735.

SAVONA.

CON·POL·DI·S·CASA

LORETO. XVII Century.
(Con polvere di Santa Casa.)

G. A. O. F.
A Di 7 di hagosto
1708

.M, A. M

PAVIA.

Uncertain Marks.

CARLO ANDROVANDI

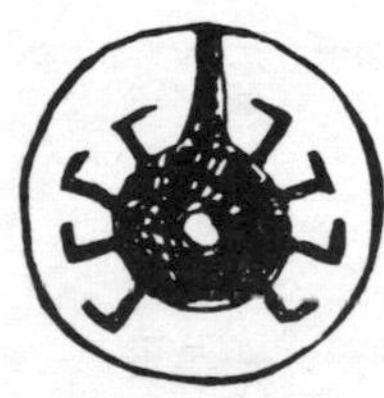

·1676

G·F G

$L

1618

VPA

IE S

·A·E·A·

1540

TÆ

FC · P. 1757

Fabrica di

Bonpencier

1547 ESIONE	GG GGL
RE MBB	I. G. S.
G L P 1667	L P
B. S. 1760	A·D·P· AC.
F.F.	P. G. 1638
F. 5 F	P.R-NP 3
G	VI f J-3-
	W. DA

Rome, 1600–1623.

SPAIN.

HISPANO MORESCO. XVI Century.
(Ill^o· Sig^r. Cardinal D'Este In Roma.)

HISPANO MORESCO. XVI Century.

MANISES. XVII Century.

HISPANO MORESCO. XVI Century.

HISPANO-MORESCO.

HISPANO MORESCO. XV Century.

SARGADELOS (Modern). XIX Century.

SEVILLE (Modern). XIX Century.

SEVILLE (Modern).
Pickman & Co. XIX Century.

SEVILLE. Pickman. XIX Century.

SEVILLE.

ALCORA.

BUEN RETIRO. Established 1769.

ALCORA. XVIII Century.

ALCORA.

MOX *Mark of José de Zaragoza*	Soliua	MIGUEL	Vilaxca
	F'o	Granzel	GROS

ALCORA.

SEGOVIA (Modern). XIX Century.

LISBON. XIX Century.

MAFRA
CALDAS
PORTUGAL

CALDAS.

Arzobispo

PUENTA DE ARZOBISPO.

M. P.

MIRAGAÏA.

PORTO.

COIMBRA.

MALTA (Modern). XIX Century.

FABRICA DE MASSARELLOS.

VIANA DE CASTELLO.

F. R.

R R

RATO.

PERSIA.

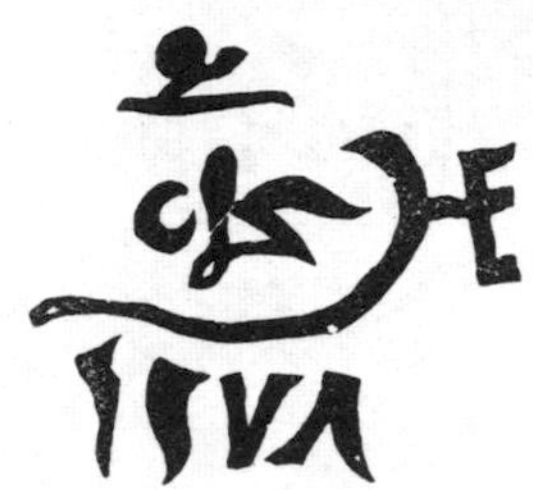

FRANCE.

OIRON (Henri II Ware). XVI Cent.
Now termed SAINT PORCHAIRE.

OIRON (Henri II Ware). XVI Cent.

OIRON. XVII Century.

I.P.S.
A LYON
1773

LYON
C.F

LYON.

ffait en decembre
Mv.XI.

BEAUVAIS. XVI Century.

BEAUVAIS. XVI Century.

J Entoine
J'englefontaine

ENGLEFONTAINE.

SARGUEMINES.
Utzchneider, established 1770.

VOISINLIEU. Ziegler, established 1839.

CREIL.

HB Cie
Choisy le Roy

CHOISY.

H B & Cie
CHOISY
LE ROI

CHOISY.

S^t C
T

ST. CLOUD. Trou, 1722.

PARIS. XVI Century. F. Briot.

OLIVIER
A PARIS.

PARIS.

AR AR AR

PARIS. XVII Century. Révérend.

PARIS. XIX Century. H. Pinart.

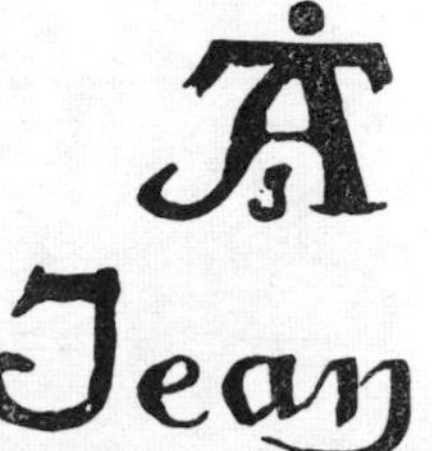

PARIS. XIX Century. A. Jean.

TD

PARIS. XIX Century. T. Deck.

PULL

OR

Pull.

PARIS.

B. V.

PARIS.
XIX Century. Victor Barbizet.

PARIS. XIX Century. Lessore.

Lessore

PARIS. XIX Century. Lessore.

Vve. DUMAS
66 *rue Fontaine-au-Roi.*
PARIS.

I. D.

PARIS. XIX Century. J. Devers.

M. Bouquet.

PARIS.

AVON. XVII Century.

E

AVON LES FONTAINEBLEAU.

P. P
a Limage N. D.
a Saintes
1680

SAINTES. XVII Century.

I.B

LA ROCHELLE.

A, MORREINE
poitiers
1752

POITIERS.

faicte le 5e May
1642
par edme briou.
demeurant a St Verain

ST. VERAIN.

I·R·PALVADEAV·
1643

NANTES.

N

NEVERS. XVII Century. N. Viode.

NEVERS.
XVII Century. Jacques Seigne.

NEVERS.

4

NEVERS. XVII Century.

J Boulard
a Neuers
1622

NEVERS.

d conrad
Aneuers

1650-1672.

H·B
1689.

NEVERS. H. Borne.

E Borne
1689

NEVERS.

Jehan Custode ff

NEVERS, 1602-60.

NEVERS. J. Bourdu, 1802-20.

DLF
1636

NEVERS. D. Le Fevre, 1636.

·P·S·
1630

NEVERS.

NEVERS. XVII Century.

NEVERS.

Claude Bigourat,

1764.

NEVERS.

F. R. 1734.

NEVERS.

Borne
Pinxit
Anno
1738

NEVERS.

HS

NEVERS.

M. MONTAIGNON. NEVERS.

TR

Marzy (Nièvre)

1855

MARZY, near NEVERS.

faict a Rouen

1647

A ROUEN

1542

Go

ROUEN. XVIII Century.

Brument

1699.

ROUEN.

ROUEN. XVII Century.

ROUEN.

ROUEN. XVIII Century.

GÆR

ROUEN. Guillebaud. XVIII Century.

D

ROUEN. XVIII Century.

ROUEN. XVIII Century.

ROUEN. XVIII Century.

ROUEN. XVIII Century.

Gardin

ROUEN. XVIII Century.

ROUEN. XVIII Century.

ROUEN. XVIII Century.

A·ROÜEN
·1725·
PEINT PAR
PIERRE
CHAPEtte

ROUEN.

Signature of Le Vavasseur in 1743.	Signatures of Guillebaud in 1730.	Signatures of Claude Borne.

Signature of N. J. Bellenger, 1800.

Initials of P. Caussy, 1720.

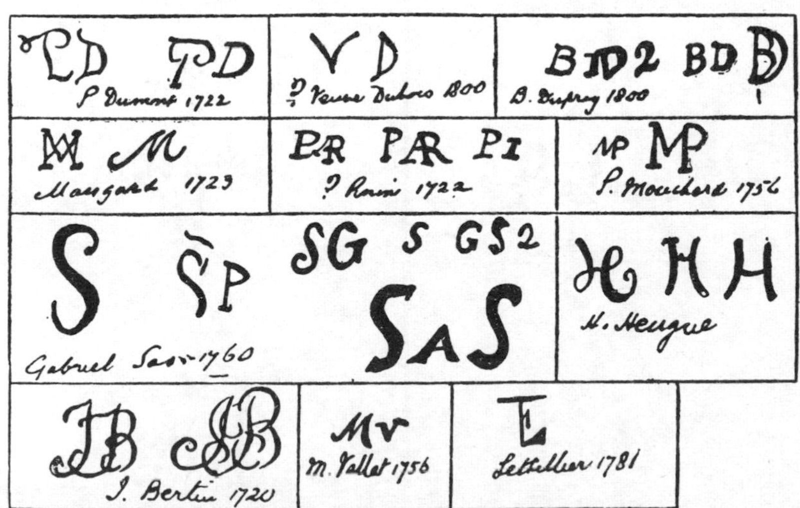

The above signatures occur on specimens of Rouen fayence.

NIDERVILLER.
Beyerlé, established 1760.

NIDERVILLER. Custine.

NIDERVILLER. Custine. XVIII Cent.

NIDERVILLER. Custine. XVIII Cent.

NIDERVILLER.

CHATEAU D'ANNET. XVII Century.

STRASBOURG. Hannong. XVIII Cent.

STRASBOURG.
J. Hannong. XVIII Century.

STRASBOURG. Hannong. XVIII Cent.

STRASBOURG.
J. Hannong. XVIII Century.

Blois. XIX Century.

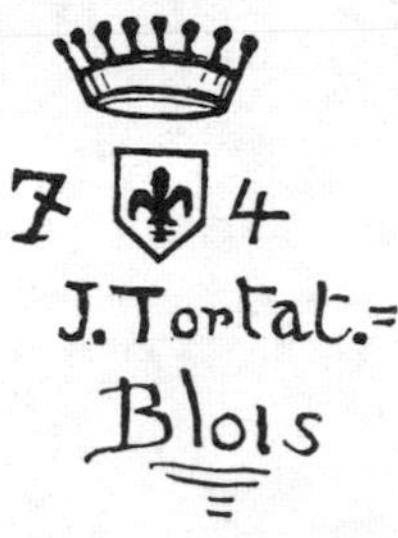

Blois

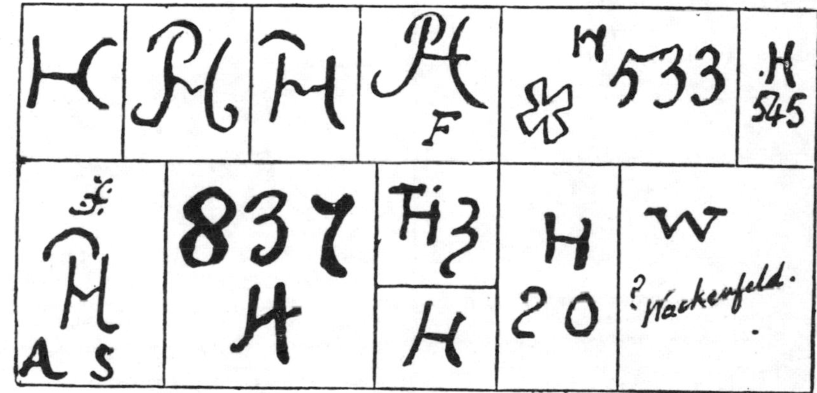

Strasbourg.

G. Viry f. a Monstiers.

chez Clerissy

Moustiers. Established 1698.

Vf

·F.e

M·C·A 1756·J·A

Soliua ca

Miguel Vilax

F o Grangel

CROS

MOUSTIERS.
Various Potters, XVII and XVIII Centuries.

MOUSTIERS. Olery.

·OY·

Sc

MOUSTIERS. XVIII Century.
Marks of Olery with Painter's Initials.

MOUSTIERS.

MOUSTIERS, 1778.

ferrat moustiers

Pierre Fournier DE Moustiers: 1775.

MOUSTIERS. Guichard, potter.

Thion à Moustiers.

Antoine Guichard,
de Moustiers, 1763,
le 10 Xbre

MOUSTIERS. XVIII Century.
Other Potters.

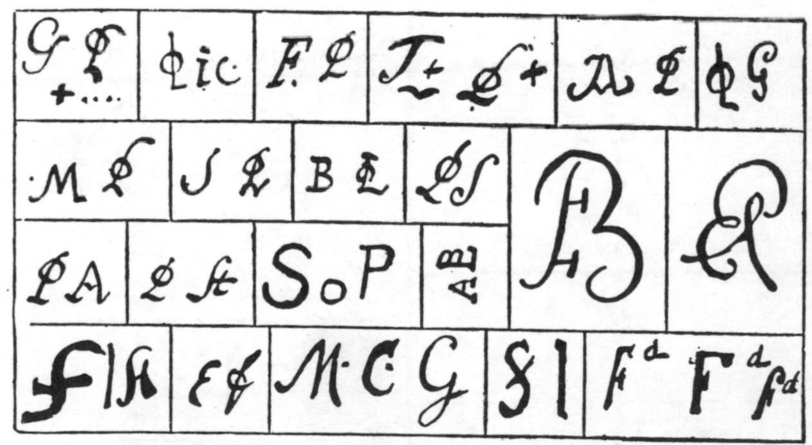

The signature of Féraud.

poupre
a japonne

POUPRES. Circa 1750.

amoulins

MOULINS. XVIII Century.

chollet ferit
de moulain
1742

estienne mogain

1741 E.M.

MOULINS.
Potter and Painters' Names.

MARAN
1754
R

M

MARANS, near ROCHELLE.

M

MONTAUBAN.

FAZ 1778
DLS

MONTAUBAN.

L L

ARDUS.

LA TOUR D'AIGUES.

APT.

GOULT.

Claude Pelisie,
1726.
VAL-SOUS-MEUDON.

M. Sansont,
1738.
VAL-SOUS-MEUDON.

VAL-SOUS-MEUDON. Metenhoft and Mourot. XVIII Century.

DESVRE. XVIII Century.
Dupré Poulaine.

Saint-Omer
1759.

ST. OMER.

"Fait par moi Laroze fils, a Sainte-Foy."

SAINTE-FOY.

VALENCIENNES.

VALENCIENNES.

VALENCIENNES.

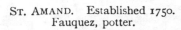

St. Amand departeman du nor.

ST. AMAND. Established 1750. Fauquez, potter.

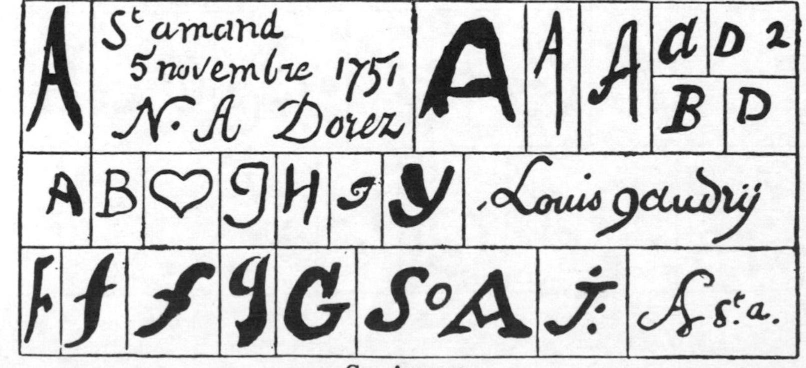

ST. AMAND.

Rouy.

ROUY.

·S· pelleré

SINCENY. Pellevé. XVIII Century.

B.T.

SINCENY.

S·

·S·

Sinchenÿ·

8 D

·S.c.ÿ.

à monsieur
monsieur Sincenÿ
a Sincenÿ
an picardis.

SINCENY, 1734–1864.

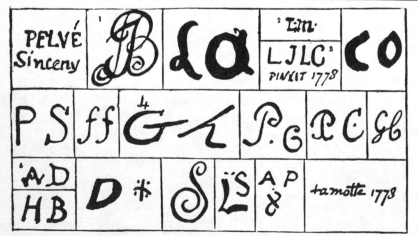

PELVÉ Sinceny	[1]	La	[2] Lm· / LJLC[3] PINXIT 1778	CO

PS	ff	[4] G	P.G	PC	Gb

[5] AD / HB	D	S	LS	AP	tamotte 1778

[1] Monogram of Jos. Bedeau. [2] Initials of L. Meériat, [3] Initials of J. Lecerf.
[4] Mark of Ghaïl. [5] Initials of A. Daussy.

LR

BORDEAUX. Lahens and Rateau, 1826.

LIMOGES. J. Pouyat, 1830.

A + Limoges
Le 18me may
J74J

LIMOGES.

C
G.

TAVERNES. Circa 1760. Gaze.

MONTPELIER.
Le Vouland. XIX Century.

V

VARAGES. XVIII Century.

faite à Martres,
18 *Septembre,*
1775.

MARTRES.

MARSEILLES, established 1607.

MARSEILLES. XVIII Century.

C°
S

MARSEILLES. XVIII Century.

MARSEILLES.

MARSEILLES.

MARSEILLES.
J. Robert. XVIII Century.

Ṙ
·R·X·

MARSEILLES. Robert.

V. Perrin

V.P.

VP

MARSEILLES. Veuve Perrin.

MARSEILLES.

B·

MARSEILLES. Bonnefoy.

MARSEILLES. Fauchier.

Jacques Borelly

MARSEILLES. XVIII Century.

Ch G.F. C° S

MARSEILLES.

MANERBE.

m
Clermont ferrand
D'auvergne
21 jãuier 1736

CLERMONT-FERRAND.

SAINT-LONGE.

SAINT-LONGES.

Clermont Ferrand
1734.

CLERMONT-FERRAND.

MEILLONAS.

CLERMONT.

CLERMONT.

Pidoux 1765
à Miliona.

MEILLONAS.

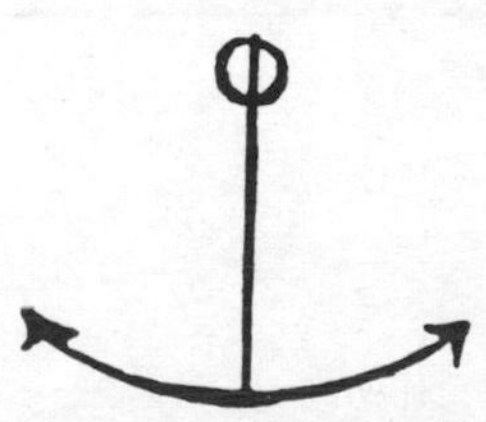

SCEAUX. Glot, 1775.

SCEAUX-PENTHIÈVRE.
Established 1753–1795.

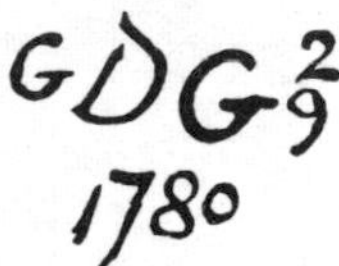

RENNES.

Castilhon.

CASTILHON.

P. A
c. aprey

APREY. Established c. 1750 by Lallemand, Baron D'Aprey.

M.

MATHAUT.

BOURG-LA-REINE.

B la R

BOURG-LA-REINE. XVIII Century.

UZES. XIX Century. F. Pichon.

P.B.C.

NISMES. XIX Century.
Plantier, Boncoirant & Co.

A.D.T.

RUBELLES, 1856. Baron de Tremblé.

H

VINCENNES. Hannong. XVIII Cent.

ORLEANS. XVIII Century.

LAUrens + Basso +
A Toulouza
Le 14ª maÿ 1756.

TOULOUSE. XVIII Century.

TOULOUSE. Fouquez, Arnoux & Co.

QUIMPER. Hubaudière, 1809.

QUIMPER.

QUIMPER. XVIII Century.

fait a tours le
21 Mair 1782
Lovis ⁘ LIAVTE

TOURS. Established 1770.

MONTET. Laurjorois. XIX Century.

TOURS. V. Avisseau. XIX Century.

avisseau
a tours
1855

TOURS.

TOURS. Landais. XIX Century.

CH. de BOISSIMON et Cie.
a LANGEAIS INDRE & LOIRE.

LANGEAIS.

Casamene, Besançon.

GIEN
Geoffroi

Gien.

J.L.

Premieres. Lavalle. XIX Century.

Premieres. Lavalle. XIX Century.

Uncertain Marks.

ALEX 1724

J:Alliot

CD
CABRI
1762

J+Jamart
1696

Jean: gony

+ Leger +
Leieune +
+ 1730 +

NIcoLasH.V
1738

1	AN
2	A P.
3	A P
4	BR
5	CB
6	·C· ·S·
7	δ
8	F
9	F.C – 1661
10	Fc 2/1 Sc
11	F E.
12	f·L·
13	GAA
14	GDG 1780 2/2
15	HA
16	HE
17	Ḣ G
18	H
19	G H
20	·II·
21	J.
22	JB
23	A·R· f
24	R
25	OIP′
26	OS
27	PB
28	P
29	P+
30	GP
31	P.R.
32	pv 3 | 2
33	R
34	R;B F
35	RL
36	R·M· f·
37	S· G· N·
38	SP
39	T.C.E 1793 an 4c
40	VM
41	W 2
42	W H
43	·P·
44	Po 5 V 1661

(The reference numbers refer to Large Edition, *vide* pp. 260, 261.)

SWEDEN. DENMARK.

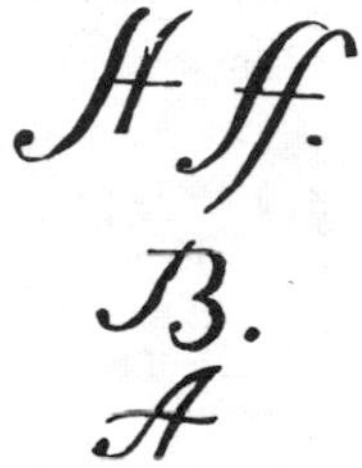

STOCKHOLM. Established 1726.

STOCKHOLM. A. Fahlstrom, painter.

STOCKHOLM. D. Hillberg, painter.

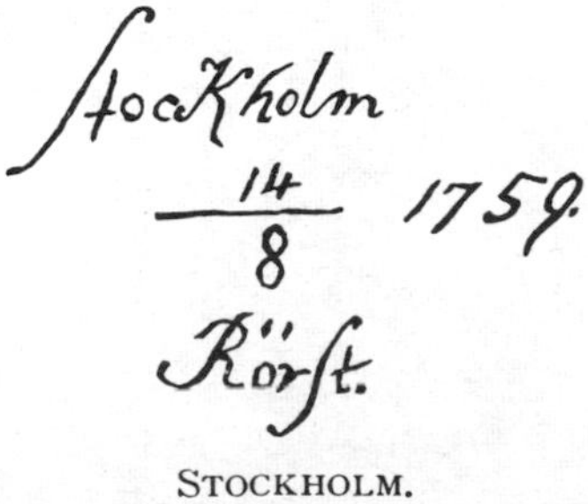

STOCKHOLM.

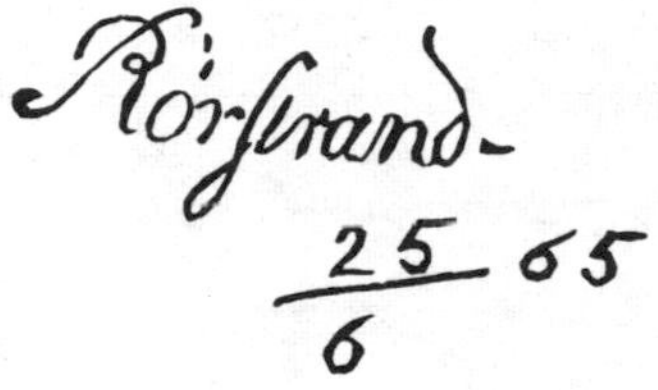

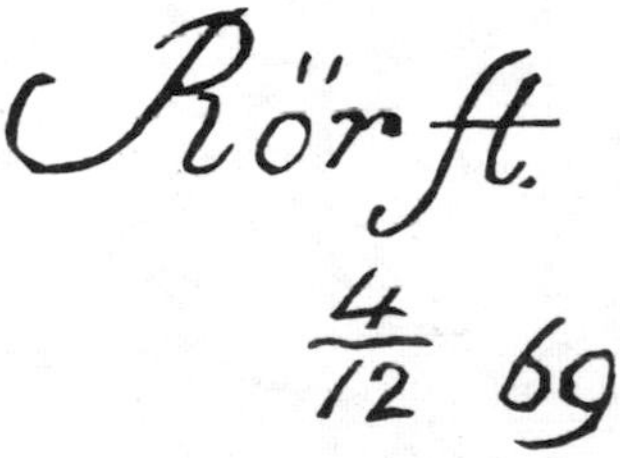

RORSTRAND & Rorstrand.
RÖRSTRAND, 1769.

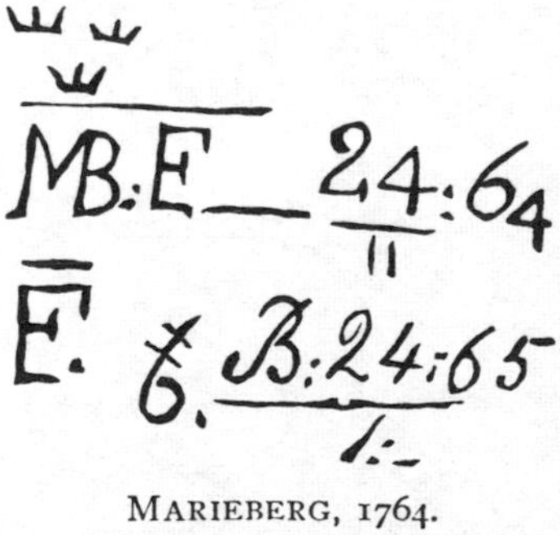

MARIEBERG, 1764.
Ehrenreich, Director. Frantzen, painter.

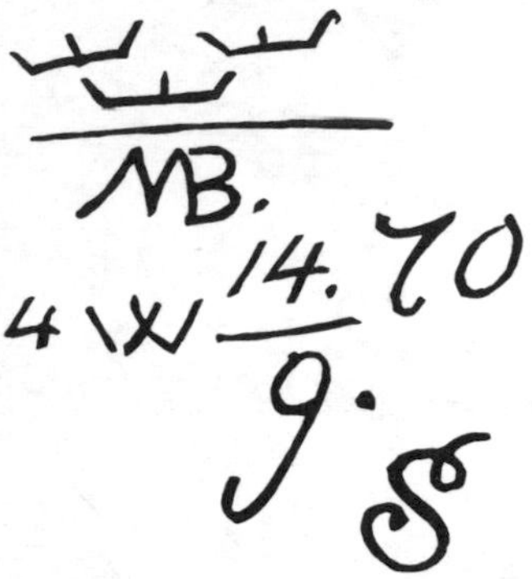

MARIEBERG. XVIII Century.
Sten, Director.

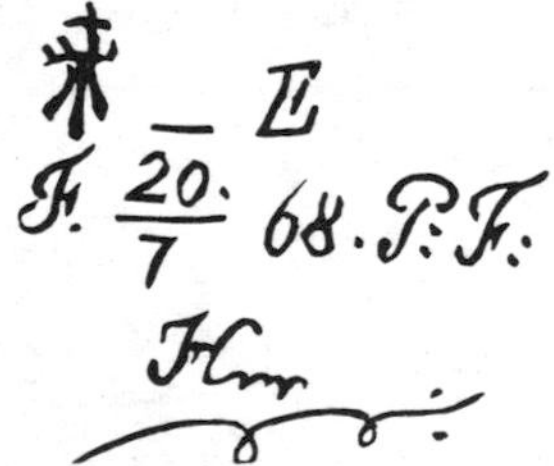

STRALSUND, 1768. Herveghr, painter.

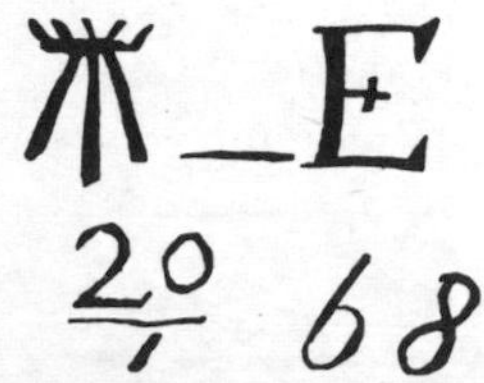

STRALSUND, 1768.
Ehrenreich, Director.

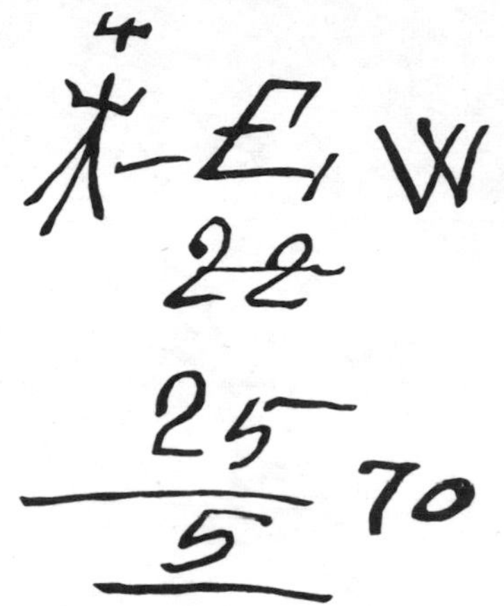

STRALSUND. Ehrenreich, 1770.

KIEL, 1769.
Buchwald, Director.
Leihammer, painter.

Kiel
Buchwald. Director:
Abr: Leihamer fecit:

KIEL. Circa 1770.

Stf
B
AL

Stockelstorff 1773
Buchwald Dirit
Abr: Leihamer fecit

STOCKELSDORF.

O
Eckernförde
Buchwald
AL 67

O
E
B
M

O
E 66
B
A

Otto
Eckernförde
Buchwald 67
Jahr

ECKERNFÖRDE.

GUSTAFSBERG

GUSTAFSBERG, 1820.

Künersberg

XVIII Century.

HELSINBERG.

XVIII Century.

KÜNERSBERG.

GERMANY.

Baÿreuthe
K Hu.

BAYREUTH. XVII Century.

BP

BAYREUTH. XVIII Century.

BK
H

BAYREUTH. XVIII Century.

H

HOLITCH. XVIII Century.

1550

NUREMBERG.

Hans Kraut
1578.

NUREMBERG.

Nurnberg
1723.
Gliier.

NUREMBERG. Gluer, artist.

Strobel:
Aº1730
d:22:10bris:

NUREMBERG. Strobel.

G. F. Greber
Anno 1729.
Nuremberg.

NUREMBERG.

Stadt Nuremberg
1724.
Strobel.

NUREMBERG.

G:Kosdenbusch.
GK:·

NUREMBERG.
XVIII Century. Potter's name.

NB. NB NB:·
K:· F 4.

NUREMBERG. XVIII Century.

Stebner
1771
d. 13 8bris

NUREMBERG. Stebner.

JA Marx
1735
JAM

N Pössinger
Anno 1725

NUREMBERG.

NUREMBERG.

Matthias
Rosa
im. Anspach

ANSPACH, BAVARIA. XVIII Century.

Ioh Schaper.

HARBURG.

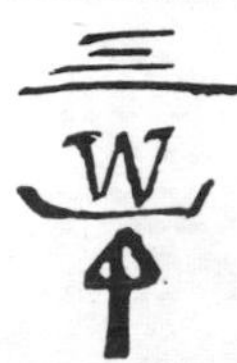

SCHREITZHEIM.

G. Manjack fecit
PROSKAU.

PROSKAU.

göggingen
HS

GOGGINGEN, BAVARIA. XVIII Cent.

POPPLESDORF. XVIII Century.
M. Wessel, potter.

HÖCHST. Established by Gelz, 1720.

HÖCHST. XVIII Century.

jZ G

HÖCHST. XVIII Century.

Zeschinger

HÖCHST. XVIII Century.

HÖCHST. Dahl. XIX Century.

MAYENCE?

DIRMSTEIN.

Pinxit J. G. Hiegel
Arnstadt d: 9 Maÿ
·1775·

ARNSTADT.

ARNSTADT. XVIII Century.

A.N.

ALTENROLHAU.
Nowotny. XVIII Century.

MORAVIA. Frain. XVIII Century.

H or H or H

FRANKENTHAL, 1754.
Paul and J. Hannong.

H
H 872

FRANKENTHAL. Hannong.

FRANKENTHAL, 1754.
Paul and J. Hannong.

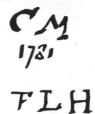

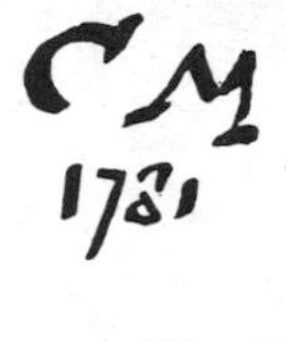

FLÖRSHEIM.

TEINITZ. XVIII Century.

ZELL.

FÜNFKIRCHEN.

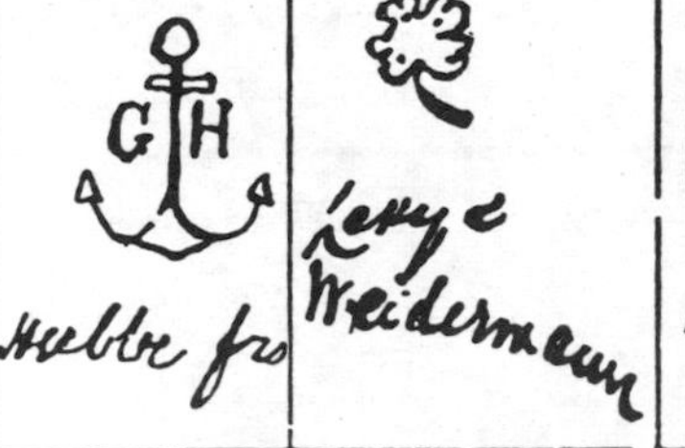

NEUHALDENSLEBEN.

SCHL ERBACH.

BONN.

KÖNIGSTEDTEN.

RÜCKINGEN.

OFFENBACH, 1739.

HORNBERG.

AMBERG.

GRUNSTADT.

WITTEBURG.

SCHWEIDNITZ.

ANNABURG.

VORDAMM.

RHEINSBERG.

DANTZIG.

LESUM.

RENDSBURG.

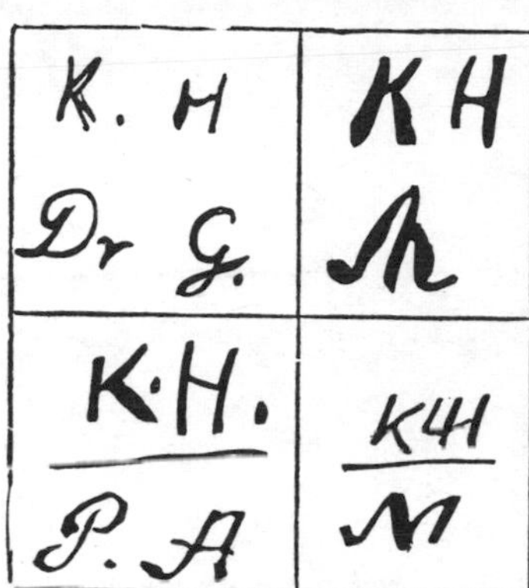

KELLINGHUSEN

GROHN.

ILMENAU.

NEUFRIEDSTEIN.

GRÄFENRODA.

DORNHEIM.

EISENACH.

MEISSEN.

AUMUND.

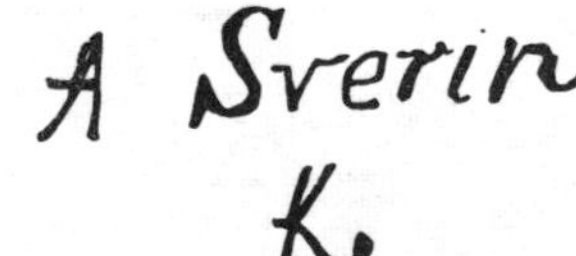

SCHWERIN.

MINDEN.

JEVER.

SCHLESWIG.

Uncertain Marks.	d: 12 8br A° 1739 Valentin Bontemps.
A. F. 1687.	LBurg. 1792.
M.D.C. 1762	GHEDT W:I:M I750
	F.B.G.F. 1779
A.B 1638	G.C.P. 1730

F: Pahl:: Ao: 1796:	N Pössinger Anno 1725

TABLE OF UNKNOWN GERMAN POTTERS' MARKS.

No.	Mark	No.	Mark	No.	Mark	No.	Mark
1	AB	9	·H.H	19	M	28	T.
2	A / P / MR	10	HE HA	20	M / 6	29	T DR
3	B / S	11	HP. / Go	21	R / N·	30	VH / 3
4	DP / 83x	12	HL	22	oAF	31	W
5	F	13	:HS:	23	PH.	32	
6	F	14	.K.	24	K / M / 67	33	b.
7	H	15	I·K	25	R·M / E	34	x a
8	H.	16	HV XX	26	S.K	35	NO
		17	L	27	KB.B	36	:HN XX
		18	L·			37	WS

SWITZERLAND.

Z

B
Z

ZURICH.

Schaphuÿsen.
Genrit Euers.

SCHAFFHAUSEN. XVI Century.

MUNSTER.

L. B

LENZBURG.

METTLACH.

HUBERTSBERG.

Unknown Marks.

F. T. 1559.

H V G.

NE
M
1589

B. V. 1574.

K° R. 1598.

L. W. 1573.

M. G. 1586.

L. W.

W. T.

R.V.H

M. O.

I. E.

I. R. 1588.

M. G. 1586.

B. M.

COLOGNE. Grès. XVI Century.

H. W.

COLOGNE. Fayence. XVIII Century.
M. L. Cremer, potter.

BELGIUM.

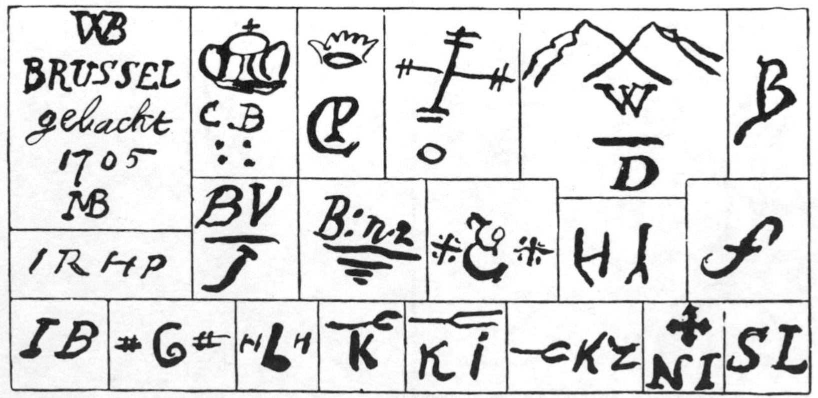

BRUSSELS.

BRUSSELS.

AD.W.

ANDENNES.
A. Vander Waert. XIX Century.

ANDENNES.
B. Lammens. XIX Century.

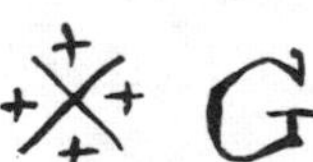

TOURNAY. XVIII Century.

BL

LUXEMBOURG. Boch. Estab^d. 1767.

LUXEMBOURG.

CCC
C.P.

LUXEMBOURG. XVIII Century.

HP

BRUGES.

BRUGES.

LILLE.

LILLE.

N : A
DOREZ
1748.

LILLE. Dorez.

Lille, 1768.

LILLE.

CAMBRAY.

LILLE.

Fecit IACOBUS FEBVRIER,
Insulis in Flandria,
Anno 1716.

Pinxit MARIA STEPHANUS
BORNE Anno 1716.
LILLE.

LILLE. F. Boussemart.

P B
B

LILLE. Boussemart.

LILLE. Masquelier.

LILLE.
Painters' Marks. Estabd. 1696–1800.

LILLE.

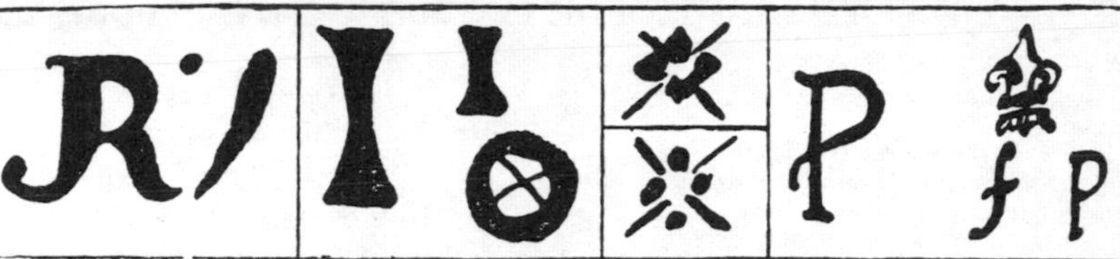

LILLE.

HOLLAND.

Gaberil Vengobechea
Houda.
HOUDA. XVIII Century.

Johann Otto Lessel
Sculpsit; et Pinxit.

Hamburg Mensis
Januarij Anno 1756

HAMBURG.

Ghemaeckte tot Belle
C. Jacobus Hennekens
anno 1717,
and inside
Belle C.I.H.
BAILLEUL.

AMSTERDAM, 1780. H. Van Laun.

LIST of POTTERS, with dates of election to the Gild of St. Luc.

1. Gerrit Hermansz, 1614.
2. Isaac Junius, 1640.
3. Albrecht de Keizer, 1642.
4. Jan Gerrits Van der Hoeve, 1649.
5. Meynaert Garrebrantsz, 1616.
6. Quiring Alders Kleynoven, 1655.
7. Frederick Van Frytom, 1658.
8. Jan Sicktis Van den Houk, 1659.
9. Jan Ariens Van Hammen, 1661.
10. Augustijn Reygens, 1663.
11. Jan Jans Kulick, 1662.
12. Jacob Cornelisz, 1662.
13. Willem Kleftijus, 1663.
14. Arij Jans de Milde, 1658.
15. Piet Vizeer, 1752.
16. Gysbert Verhaast, 1760.
17. Arend de Haak, 1780.
18. Dirk Van Schie, 1679.
19. Pieter Poulisse, 1690.
20. Lucas Van Dale, 1692.
21. Cornelis Van der Kloot, 1695.
22. Jan Baan, 1660.
23. Jan Decker, 1698.
24. Arij Cornelis Brouwer, 1699.
25. Leonardus of Amsterdam, 1721.
26. Paulus Van der Stroom, 1725.

De Metale Pot.

27. Jeronimus Pieters Van Kessel, 1655.
28. Lambertus Cleffius, 1678.
29. Lambartus Van Eenhoorn, 1691.
30. Factory mark.

De Griekse A.

31. Gisbrecht Lambrecht Kruyk, 1645.
32. Samuel Van Eenhoorn, 1674.
33. Adrianus Kocks, 1687.
34. Jan Van der Heul, 1701.
35. Jan Theunis Dextra. 1759.
36. Jacobus Halder, 1765.

De Dubbelde Schenkkan.

37. Factory mark (D.S.K.).
38. Ambrensie Van Kessel, 1675.
39. Louis Fictoor, 1689.
40. Hendrik de Koning, 1721.

T'Hart.

41. Factory mark.
42. Matheus Van Boegart, 1734.
43. Hendrik Van Middeldyk, 1764.

De Paaw.

44. Factory mark, 1651.

T'Oude Moriaans Hofft.

45. Rochus Jacobs Hoppestein, 1680.
46. Antoni Kruisweg, 1740.
47. Geertruij Verstelle, 1764.

De Klaew.

48. Lambertus Sanderus, 1764.

De Boot.

49. Dirk Van der Kest, 1698.
50. Johannes den Appel, 1759.

De Drie Klokken.

51. Usual mark (three bells), 1671.

De Romeyn.

52. Reinier Hey, 1696.
53. Japanese characters.
54. Japanese characters.
56. Petrus Van Marum, 1759.
57. Johannes Van der Kloot, 1764.

De 3 Porceleyne Flessies.

58. Tripartite mark of Cornelis de Keizer and Jacob and Adrian Pynacker, 1680.
59. Adrian Pynacker, 1690.

De Drie Astonnen.

60. G. Pieters Kam, 1674.
61. Factory mark.
62. Zachariah Dextra, 1720.
63. Hendrick Van Hoorn, 1759.

De Porceleyne Schotel.

64. Johannes Pennis, 1725.
65. Jan Van Duijn, 1760.

De Roos.

66 and 67. Factory marks, 1675.
68. Dirck Van der Does, 1759.

De Porceleyne Bijl.

69. Factory mark, 1679–1776.

De Porceleyne Fles.

70. Johannes Knotter, 1698.
71. Pieter Van Doorne, 1759.

De Star.

72. Factory mark.
73. Cornelis de Berg, 1690.
74. Jan Aalmes, 1731.
75. Justus de Berg, 1759.
76. Abertus Kiell, 1763.

T'Fortuin.

77, 78, and 79. Factory marks, 1691.
80 and 81. Paul Van der Briel, 1740.

De Verguld Blompot.

82. Factory mark, 1693.
83. Matheus Van Bogaert.
84. Pieter Verburg.

De Twee Wildemans.

85. Willem Van Beek, 1713–1758.

De Twee Schepjes.

86. Anthony Pennis, 1759.

T'Jongue Moriaan's Hofft.

87. Johannes Verhagen, 1728.

De Lampetkan.

88. Gerrit Brouwer, 1756.
89. Abram Van der Keel, 1780.

Discontinued about 1813.

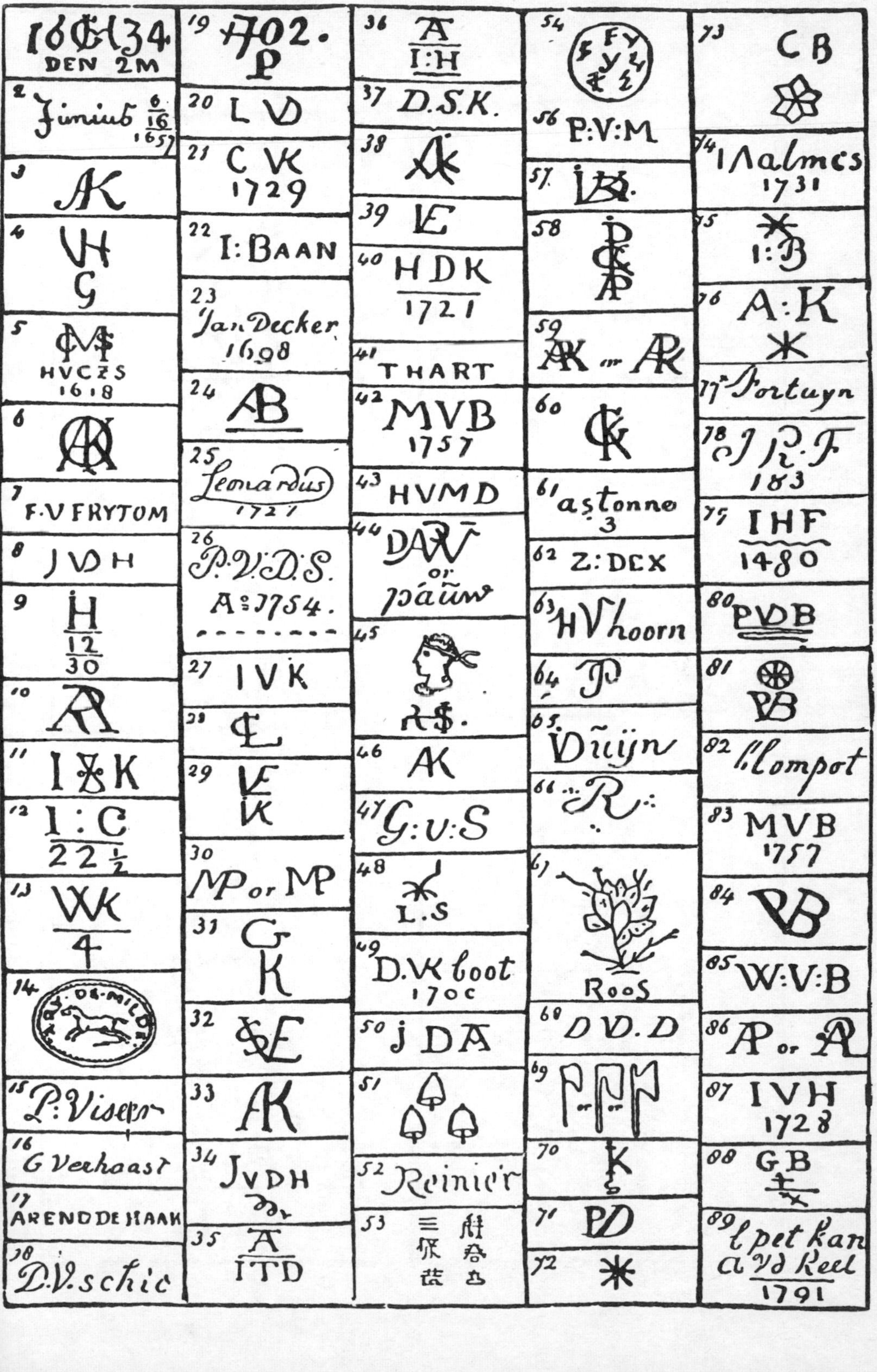

1. 16 (H 34 DEN 2M
2. Junius 6/16/1657
3. AK
4. VH G
5. CM$ HVCZS 1618
6. AOK
7. F.V FRYTOM
8. JVDH
9. H 12/30
10. AR
11. I8K
12. I:C 22½
13. WK 4
14. VAN DE MILDE
15. P: Visear
16. G Verhoast
17. ARENDDEHAAK
18. D.V.schie
19. 1702. P
20. LVD
21. CVK 1729
22. I: BAAN
23. Jan Decker 1698
24. AB
25. Leonardus 1727
26. P.V.D.S. A°1754.
27. IVK
28. CL
29. VE VK
30. MP or MP
31. G K
32. SE
33. AK
34. JVDH
35. A ITD
36. A I:H
37. D.S.K.
38. AK
39. VE
40. HDK 1721
41. THART
42. MVB 1757
43. HVMD
44. DAW or pauw
45. [head] AS.
46. AK
47. G:V:S
48. [illegible] L.S
49. D.VK boot 1700
50. j DA
51. [bells]
52. Reinier
53. [illegible]
54. [illegible]
56. P:V:M
57. IVB
58. PCKAP
59. AK or AR
60. CK
61. astonne 3
62. Z: DEX
63. HV hoorn
64. P
65. Duijn
66. R
67. Roos
68. DVD.D
69. [illegible]
70. K
71. PD
72. [star]
73. CB
74. I Aalmes 1731
75. I:B
76. A:K
77. Fortuyn
78. J R F 183
79. IHF 1480
80. PVDB
81. [wheel] PB
82. Compot
83. MVB 1757
84. PB
85. W:V:B
86. AP or AR
87. IVH 1728
88. GB
89. l pet kan a vd Keel 1791

Delft 1000 D P	*C. Zachtleven Fa.* 1650.
D.V.X.I	
	J.V.L 1773
D	AVH D 7 M Z D 1773
I	
IE	AIB ANNO 1774
1629 AF	C.D.G.
	GDG 1779
I·D·P 1698	D.M
	I. G. V 1768
H.S.I R	W.D.

BP	HvS 1781
I G	VIB✱
D	K
M.Q.	I Kruwzt 1775
R.T.C	Aalmes 1731
A.I.1663.	
SM. 1725.	
D / 18	
W	
VRH	AVP 1719 8 16
H·	
BFS	

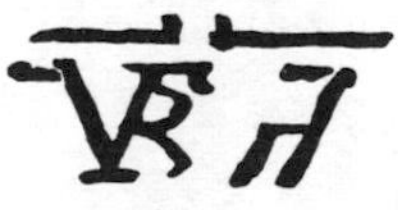

Johann Deobalt Frantz
1724

Heindering Waanders
1781.

R
R÷I
1765

HDK
13
11

R

DRX
5

AK

PDWT
1700

:*B

CHINESE DYNASTIES.

(READING FROM LEFT TO RIGHT.)

東漢	*Tung-han.*	A.D. 25.
後漢	*Hou-han.*	A.D. 221.
晉	*Tsin.*	A.D. 264.
東晉	*Tung-tsin.*	A.D. 317.
北宋	*Pei-sung.*	A.D. 420.
齊	*Chi.*	A.D. 479.
梁	*Leang.*	A.D. 502.
晉	*Tsin.*	A.D. 557.
隋	*Sui.*	A.D. 589.
唐	*Tang.*	A.D. 618.
後梁	*Hou-leang.*	A.D. 907.
後唐	*Hou-tang.*	A.D. 924.
後晉	*Hou-tsin.*	A.D. 936.
後漢	*Hou-han.*	A.D. 947.
後周	*Hou-chao.*	A.D. 951.
宋	*Sung.*	A.D. 960.
南宋	*Nan-Sung.*	A.D. 1127.
元	*Yuan* (Tartar).	A.D. 1279.
大明	*Ta-ming.*	A.D. 1368.
大清	*Tai-thsing.*	A.D. 1644.

EXAMPLES.

化 大 年 明 製 成	*Ta-ming tching-hoa nien-tchi.*
年 宣 大 製 德 明	*Ta-ming siouen-te nien-tchi.*
nien 年 *tchi* 製	During the period.

SUNG DYNASTY.

NAMES OF PERIODS.

景德	*King-te.*	A.D. 1004.
大中祥符	*Tai-chung-hsiang-fu.*	A.D. 1007.
天聖	*Tien-shing.*	A.D. 1023.
明道	*Ming-tao.*	A.D. 1023.
景祐	*Ching-yu.*	A.D. 1023.
嘉祐	*Chia-yu.*	A.D. 1023.
寶元	*Pao-yuan.*	A.D. 1023.
治平	*Chi-ping.*	A.D. 1064.
熙寧	*Hsi-ning.*	A.D. 1068.
元豐	*Yuan-fung.*	A.D. 1068.
元祐	*Yuan-yu.*	A.D. 1086.
紹聖	*Thao-shing.*	A.D. 1086.
元符	*Yuan-fu.*	A.D. 1086.
宣和	*I-ho.*	A.D. 1101.

重和	*Chung-ho.*	A.D. 1101.
政和	*Cheng-ho.*	A.D. 1101.
建中	*Chien-Chung.*	A.D. 1101.
靖國	*Ching-huo.*	A.D. 1101.
崇寧	*Tsung-ning.*	A.D. 1101.
大觀	*Ta-chuan.*	A.D. 1120.
靖康	*Ching-kang.*	A.D 1120.

NAN-SUNG DYNASTY.

NAMES OF PERIODS.

建炎	*Chien-tan.*	A.D. 1127.
紹興	*Shao-hsing.*	A.D. 1127.
隆興	*Lung-hsing.*	A.D. 1163.
乾道	*Chien-tao.*	A.D. 1163.
淳熙	*Tun-hsi.*	A.D. 1163.
紹熙	*Shao-hsi.*	A.D. 1190.
慶元	*Ching-yuan.*	A.D. 1195.
嘉泰	*Chia-tai.*	A.D. 1195.

開禧	*Kai-yu.*	A.D. 1195.
嘉定	*Kia-ting.*	A.D. 1195.
寶慶	*Pao-ching.*	A.D. 1225.
紹定	*Shao-ting.*	A.D. 1225.
端平	*Tuan-ping.*	A.D. 1225.
嘉熙	*Hai-hsi.*	A.D. 1225.
咸淳	*Hsien-tun.*	A.D. 1265.
德祐	*Te-yu.*	A.D. 1275.
景炎	*Ching-tan.*	A.D. 1277.
祥興	*Cheang-hsing.*	A.D. 1278.

YUAN DYNASTY.

(TARTAR).

NAMES OF PERIODS.

至元	*Chi-yuan.*	A.D. 1279.
元貞	*Yuan-tso.*	A.D. 1295.
大德	*Ta-te.*	A.D. 1295.
至大	*Chi-ta.*	A.D. 1308.
延祐	*Cheng-yu.*	A.D. 1312.
皇慶	*Huang-ching.*	A.D. 1312.
至治	*Chi-yu.*	A.D. 1321.
泰定致和	*Tai-ting chi-ho.*	A.D. 1324.
天曆	*Tien-li.*	A.D. 1329.
至順	*Chi-shan.*	A.D. 1330.
元統	*Yuan-tung.*	A.D. 1333.
至元	*Chi-yuan.*	A.D. 1333.
至正	*Chi-cheng.*	A.D. 1333.

TA-MING DYNASTY.

NAMES OF PERIODS AND EMPEROR.

洪武	*Houng-wou.*	1368.	Tai-tsou.
建文	*Kian-wen.*	1399.	Chu-ty.
永樂	*Young-lo.*	1403.	Tching-tsou.
洪熙	*Houng-hi.*	1425.	Jin-tsoung.
宣德	*Siouen-te.*	1426.	Hiouan-tsoung.
正統	*Tching-tung.*	1436.	Ying-tsoung.

景泰	*King-tai.* 1450. King-tai.
天順	*Tien-chun.* 1457. Ying-tsoung.
成化	*Tching-hoa.* 1465. Tchun-ti.
弘治	*Houng-tchi.* 1488. Hiao-tsoung.
正德	*Tching-te.* 1506. Wou-tsoung.
嘉靖	*Kia-tsing.* 1522. Chi-tsoung.
隆慶	*Loung-khing.* 1567. Mou-tsoung.
萬曆	*Wan-li.* 1573. Chin-tsoung.
泰昌	*Tai-tchang.* 1620. Kouang-tsoung
天啓	*Tien-ki.* 1621. Tchy-ti.
崇禎	*Tsoung-tsu.* 1628. Hoai-tsoung.
順治	*Chun-tchi.* 1644. Chi-tsou.
弘光	*Tsoung-kwang.* 1644.
紹武	*Tschao-wou.* 1646.
隆武	*Loung-wou.* 1646. Thang-wang.
永曆	*Yung-ly.* 1647. Kouei-wang.

TAI-THSING DYNASTY.

NAMES OF PERIODS AND EMPEROR.

天命	*Tien-ming.* 1616. Tai-tsou.
天聰	*Tien-tsoung.* 1627. Tai-tsoung.
崇德	*Tsoung-te.* 1636. Tsoung-te.
康熙	*Khang-hi.* 1662. Ching-tsou.
雍正	*Yung-tching.* 1723. Chi-tsoung.
乾隆	*Khien-long.* 1736. Koa-tsoung.
嘉慶	*Kia-king.* 1796. Jin-tsoung.
道光	*Tao-kouang.* 1821. Meen-ning.
咸豐	*Hien-fong.* 1851.
同治	*Tung-tchi.* 1862.
光緒	*Kouang-shiu.* 1875.

SEALS (*Siao-tchouan*) XV TO XIX CENTURIES.

King-te. A.D. 1004–1008.

Khang-hi. A.D. 1662–1722.

Young-lo. A.D. 1403–1425.

Yung-tching. A.D. 1723–1736.

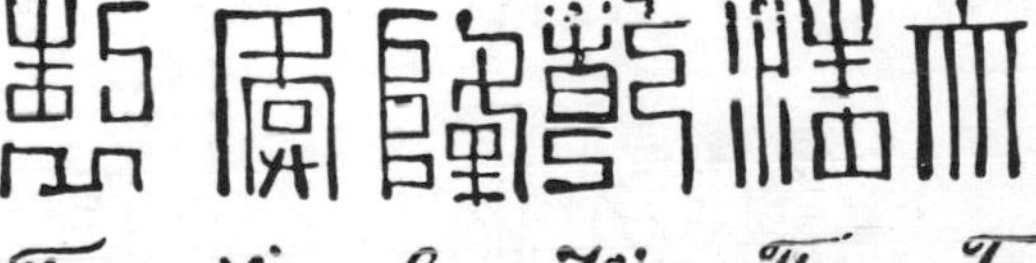

Tchy Nien Long Kien Thsing Ta

Siouen-te. A.D. 1426–1436.

Kien-long. A.D. 1736–1795.

Chun-tchi. A.D. 1644.

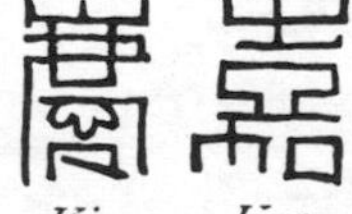

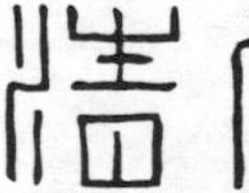

Tchi Nien King Kea Thsing Ta

Tschao-wou. A.D. 1646.

Kea-king. A.D. 1795–1821.

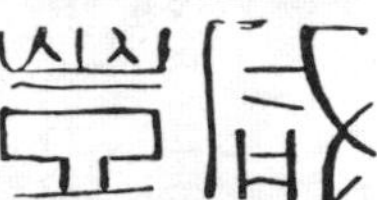

Tao-kouang. A.D. 1821–1851.

Hien-fong. A.D. 1851–1862.

Tung-tche. A.D. 1862–1875.

Fuh-kwei-kia-ki.
"A vase for the rich and honourable."

I-Shing.
"Harmonious prosperity."

Io-Shin Chin-tsang.
"Deep like a treasury of gems."

Koh-ming-tsiang-chi.
Name of maker.

Heac-chuh Choo-jin-tsaou.
"Made for the Lord of the Heae Bamboos."

Modern. Copied at Worcester.

Seal of a Mandarin.

Show or *Cheou.*
"Longevity."

Another variety or *Cheou.*

Cheou.
Another more ornamental.

景泰年製

King-te. 1450–1457.

Not deciphered.

大明宣德年製

Siouen-te. 1426–1436.

A stamp on a bronze toad.

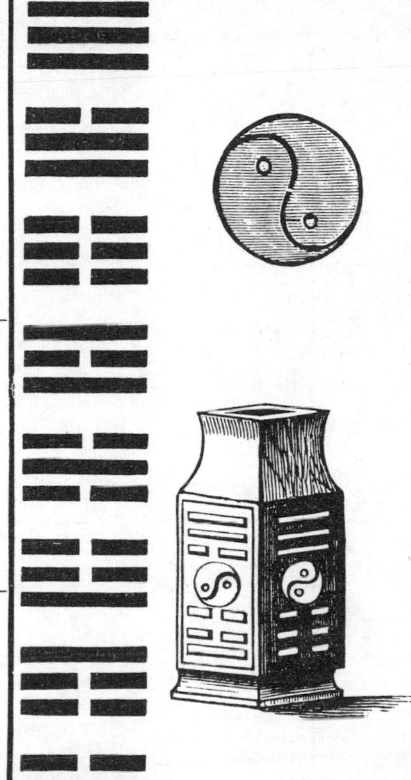

The *Pa-kwa*, or eight trigrams of Fou-hi, by which he and his followers, as we are informed, attempt to account for all the changes and transmutations which take place in nature.

Tsang-kie was the inventor of the first characters, and Fou-hi, 3468 years B.C., first traced the *Pa-kwa*—the eight symbols here given, so frequently seen on square vases—in relief, accompanied by the circular ornament, composed apparently of two fish, which forms the centre of two trigrams on each side of the vase. These Buddhist symbols were also introduced by the Japanese in their decorative wares.

No. 1. Stems.		No. 2. The Five Elements.				No. 3. Branches.
1. 甲	*Kia*	Correspond to	木	Wood.		1. 子
2. 乙	*Yih*					2. 丑
3. 丙	*Ping*	,, ,,	火	Fire.		3. 寅
4. 丁	*Ting*					4. 卯
5. 戊	*Wu*	,, ,,	土	Earth.		5. 辰
6. 己	*Ki*					6. 巳
7. 庚	*Keng*	,, ,,	金	Metal.		7. 午
8. 辛	*Sin*					8. 未
9. 壬	*Jen*	,, ,,	水	Water.		9. 申
10. 癸	*Kwei*					10. 酉
						11. 戌
						12. 亥

年製 All these inscriptions may be known as dates by the characters which usually terminate the inscription: *Nien*, year; and *tchi*, to make, form, or fashion.

年造 Sometimes other characters are used: *Nien-tsaou*, made in the year indicated.

Wo-shin-nien Leang-ki-shoo. "Painting of Leang-ki in the *Wo-shin* year." The fifth year of the seventy-fifth cycle, A.D. 1808.

卣	*Yew.* A wine cup.	尊	*Tsun.* Wine jug.
鼎	*Ting.* *Vase.*	彝	

THE SEVENTY-SIXTH SEXAGENARY CYCLE,

COMMENCING A.D. 1864.

From "Mayers' Chinese Reader's Manual."

甲子	1	己卯	16	甲午	31	己酉	46
乙丑	2	庚辰	17	乙未	32	庚戌	47
丙寅	3	辛巳	18	丙申	33	辛亥	48
丁卯	4	壬午	19	丁酉	34	壬子	49
戊辰	5	癸未	20	戊戌	35	癸丑	50
己巳	6	甲申	21	己亥	36	甲寅	51
庚午	7	乙酉	22	庚子	37	乙卯	52
辛未	8	丙戌	23	辛丑	38	丙辰	53
壬申	9	丁亥	24	壬寅	39	丁巳	54
癸酉	10	戊子	25	癸卯	40	戊午	55
甲戌	11	己丑	26	甲辰	41	己未	56
乙亥	12	庚寅	27	乙巳	42	庚申	57
丙子	13	辛卯	28	丙午	43	辛酉	58
丁丑	14	壬辰	29	丁未	44	壬戌	59
戊寅	15	癸巳	30	戊申	45	癸亥	60

NUMERALS ADOPTED BOTH IN CHINA AND JAPAN.

	Chinese Ordinary Numerals.	Pronunciation.	Chinese Merchants' Numerals.	
One . . .	一	*Yĭh*	〡	One
Two . . .	二	*Urh*	〢	Two
Three . .	三	*San*	〣	Three
Four . . .	四	*Szè*	〤	Four
Five . . .	五	*Ngôo*	〥	Five
Six . . .	六	*Lyeù*	〦	Six
Seven . .	七	*Ts'hih*	〧	Seven
Eight . .	八	*Păh*	〨	Eight
Nine . . .	九	*Kew*	〩	Nine
Ten . . .	十	*Shih*	〸	Ten
A hundred .	百	*Pŭh*	〹	Twenty
A thousand .	千	*Ts'hyen*	〺	Thirty
Ten thousand .	萬	*Wan*	〤十	Forty
			〥十	Fifty

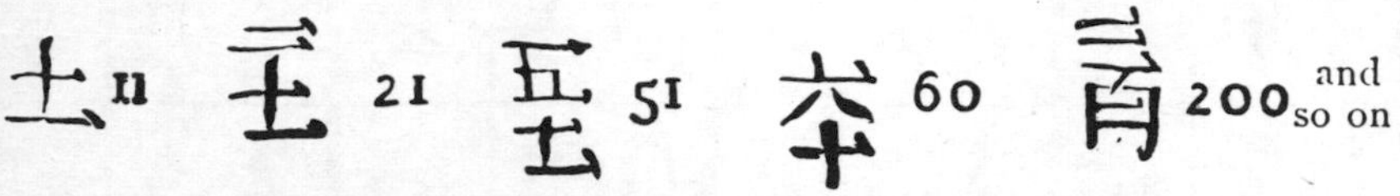

十一 11 廿一 21 五十一 51 六十 60 二百 200 and so on

INSCRIPTIONS ON CHINESE PORCELAIN.

仁和館

Jin-ho-kouan. "House of Humanity and Concord." 1111–1125.

樞府窯

Tchou-fou-yao. "Porcelain of the palace." 1260–1367.

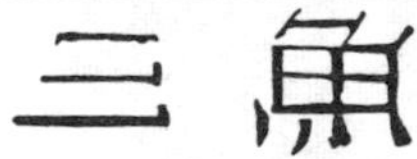

"Three fishes." Siouen-te period.

三果

"Three fruits." 1426–1435.

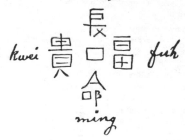

三芝

"Three mushrooms." 1426–1435.

五福

The word "Happiness" repeated five times.

Cheou. "Longevity." 1426–1435.

Thsieou. "Wine." 1521–1566.

棗湯

Tsao-t'ang. "Jujubes." 1522–1566.

薑湯

Kiang-t'ang. "Ginger." 1522–1566.

壺隱道人

Ou-in-tao-jin. "The old man who lives in solitude." 1567–1619.

chang
長
kwei 貴 口 富 fuh
命
ming

"Happiness, riches, and long life." The five blessings

五福

Woo-fuh. "The five blessings."

五福臨門

Woo-fuh-lin-mun. "May the five blessings enter here."

長富
春貴

Fuh-kouey-tchang-tchun. "Riches, high rank, and long life."

山南比壽
海東如福

Cheou-pi-uan-chan.
Fou-jou-toung-hai.

Tching-ling-kiun. Vase used at feasts.

Tchouan-youen-ki-ti. "May you obtain that title."

Ing-chin-youei. "Souvenir."

"Me! I am the friend of him."

Cheng-yeou-ya-tsi. "A distinguished reunion of friends."

Pou-kou-tchin-ouan. "Antiquarian curiosities."

Ouan-yu. "Precious jade."

Tchin-ouan. "Precious pearl."

Tai-yu. Pâte de jade.

Khi-tchin-jou-ou. "Rare as the five precious things."

Tchoui-ouan. "Precious offer."

Fou-kouei-kia-khi. "Vase for noble use."

Yu-thang-kia-khi. "A vase of the Hall of Jade."

Ting-chi-tchin-khi-chi-pao. "A rare and precious stone."

Khi-yu-thang-tchi. "Made in the Hall of Jade."

Tse-thse-thang-tchi. "Made in the Hall of the Violet Thorn."

Tchi-thang-youen-fou. "Made in the Hall of the Source of Happiness."

Tchi-thang-hien-mao. "Made in the veiled Celestial Hall."

Yu-ya-kin-hoa. "Splendid as gold in the House of Jade."

Yu-kuou-tien-tsing. "When the rain ceases, clouds become clear."

Pei-tching-tien-kien-ki-tsao. "Made by Kien-ki."

Ming Dynasty.

Thsing Dynasty.

Jade.

Pearl.

Seal of the Ming Dynasty.

A mark on porcelain.

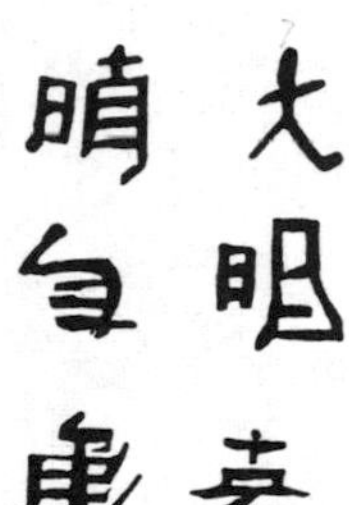

Ming Dynasty.

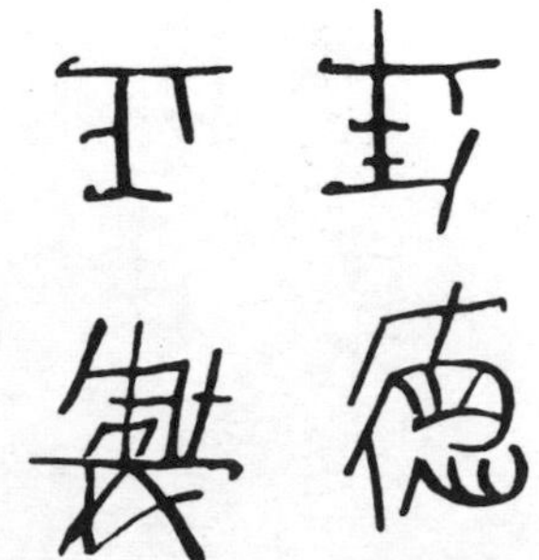

Tching-te-nien-tchi. 1506–1522.

DEVICES

FOUND ON PORCELAIN.

Wan-tse. The Creation.

Pearl. Emblem of talent.

A sonorous stone.

A stone of honour.

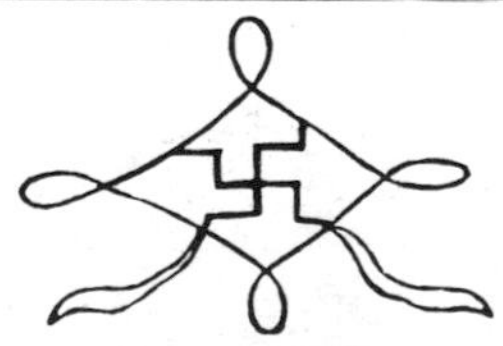

A stone of honour.

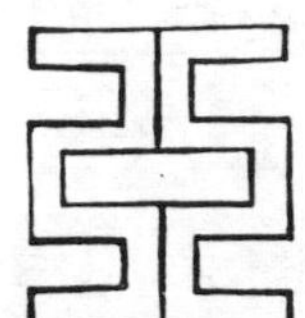

The sacred axe.

Writing implements.

Musical instruments.

A rabbit.

Choang-yu. Two fish.

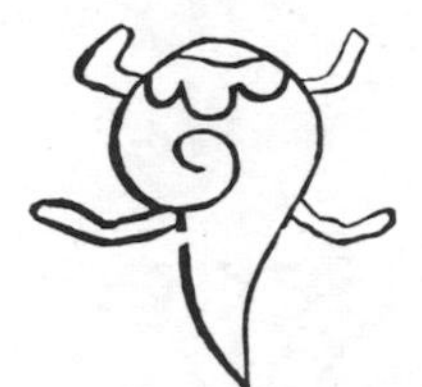

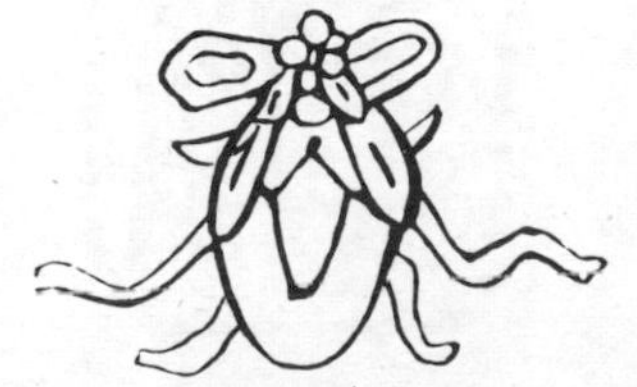

Unknown marks.

Unknown marks.

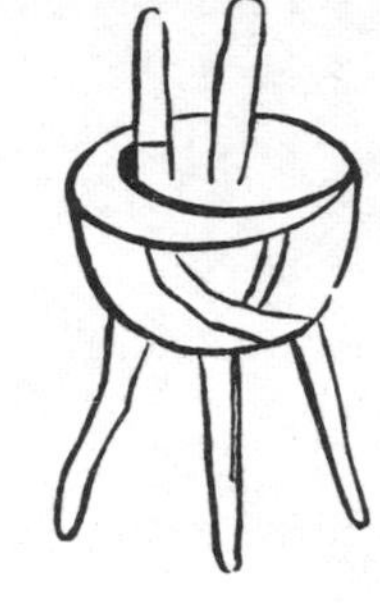

Unknown marks.

MARKS ON SPECIMENS IN THE JAPANESE PALACE, DRESDEN.

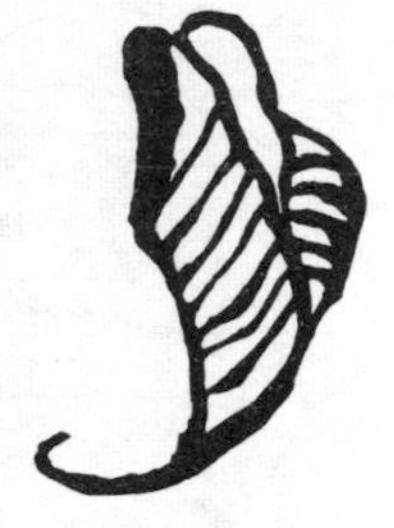

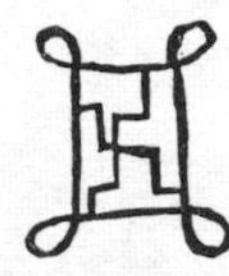

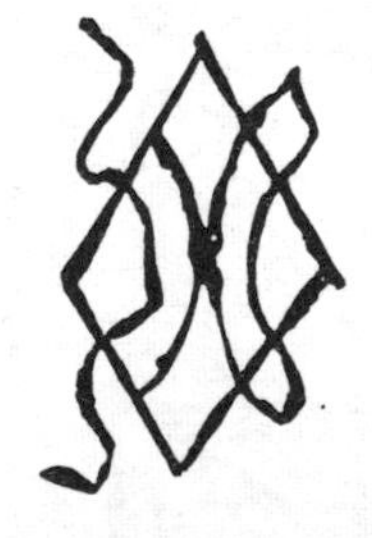

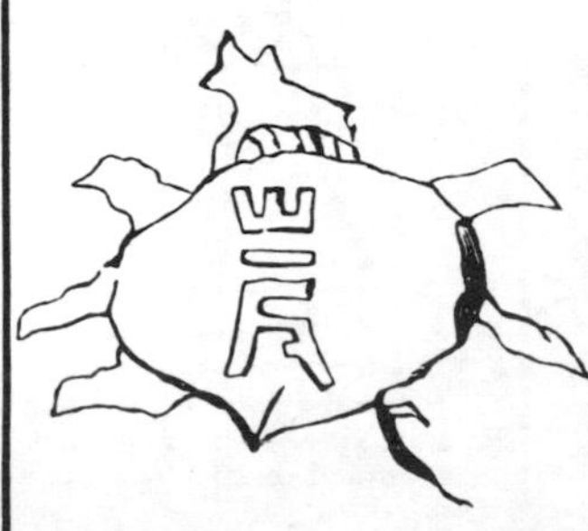

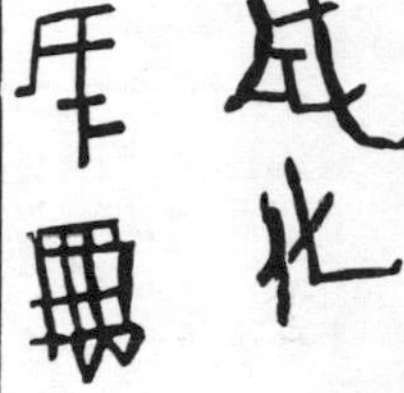

Fa. "Prosperous."

A gourd, an emblem of longevity.

Unknown.

Unknown; probably Siamese.

*

*

* Two varieties of four-legged vases with a high ear on each side. This mark has been copied on Derby porcelain, and been wrongly described as a modelling table.

戊辰年良記志	*Woshin-nien Leang-ki-shoo.* "Painting of Leang-ki in the Woshin year," the fifth year of the cycle, probably 1808.
養和堂製	*Yang-ho-tang-tchi.* "Made at the Yang-ho (encouragement of harmony) Hall."
玉堂佳器	*Yuh-tang-kea-ke.* "Beautiful vessel of the Jade Hall" (name given to the Imperial Chinese Academy).
南川錦玉	*Nan-chuen-kin-yuh.* "The elegant Jade of Nan-chuen."
師府公用	*Shwai-fuh-kung-yung.* "For the public use of the general's Hall."
聖友雅集	*Shing-yew-ya-chi.* "The elegant collection of the holy friends."
愛蓮珍賞	*Gae-lëen-chin-chang.* "Precious reward for the lover of Nelubium" (water lily).
西玉	See *Yuh.* "Western Jade."
友來	*Yew-lai.* "The arrival of friends."
宝勝	*Pao-shing.* "Inexpressibly precious."
丹桂	*Tau-kwei.* "Red olive."
	A form of the seal character, *show,* "Longevity." Known in Holland as the spider mark.

GREAT JAPAN.

DAI

NI-

PON.

Guikmon. Chrysanthemum. An Imperial mark.

Kirimon. A flower used by the Mikado as an emblem.

MINAMOTO.

MINAMOTO. Used by the Sioguns, 1593.

REGENT OF GOTAIRO, killed 1860.

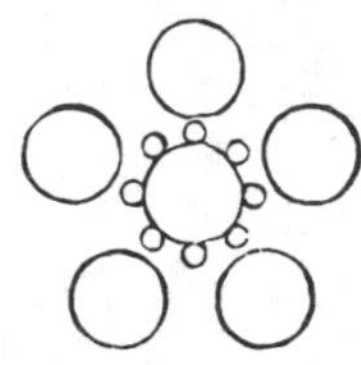

PRINCE OF KANGA.

PRINCE OF SATSUMA.

PRINCE OF SHENDAI.

NAGATO.

The Daïmios.

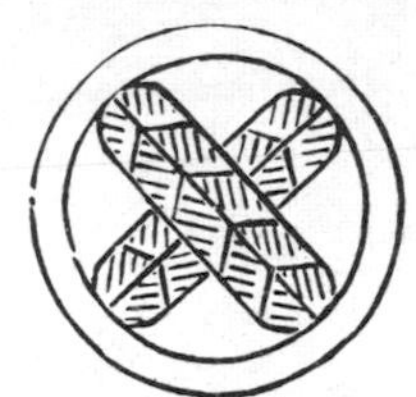
Aki.

Bizen.

Arima.

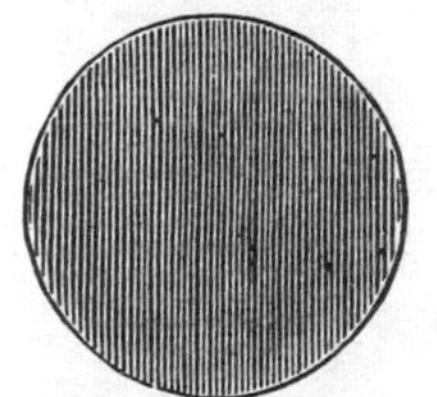
Kouroda.

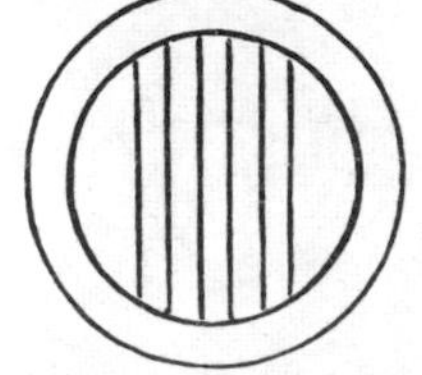
Simosa.

Daïmios.

Wakasa.

Tanga.

Ossoumi.

Yamasiro.

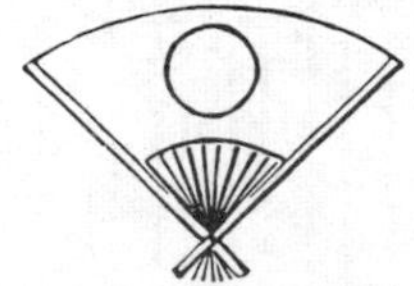
Sataké.

Daïmios.

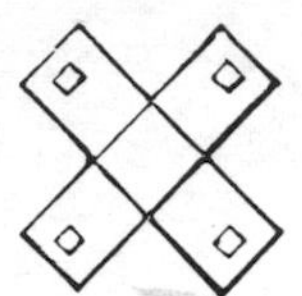

Souwô.

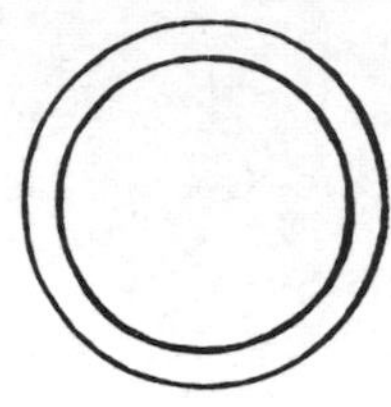

Kuwana.

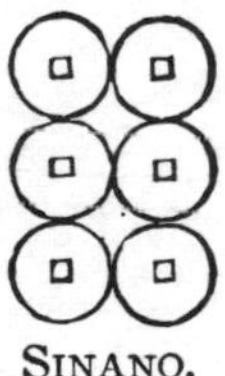

Sinano.

Asiu.

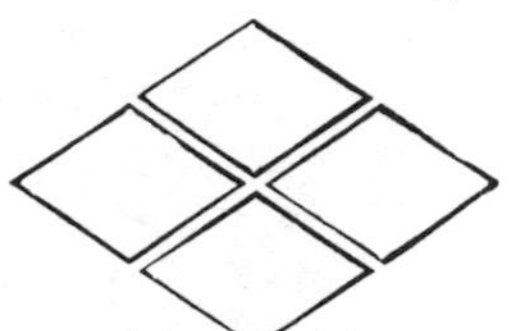

Nanbu.

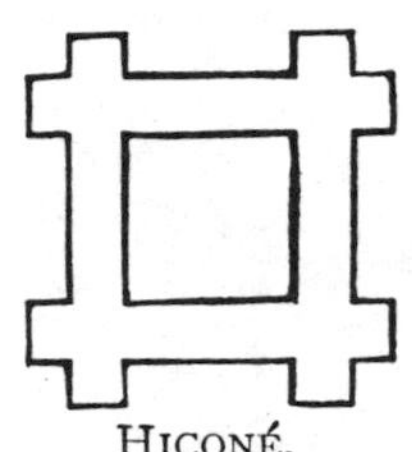

Hiconé.

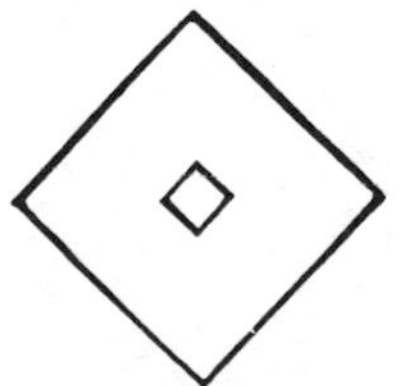

Tsikugo.

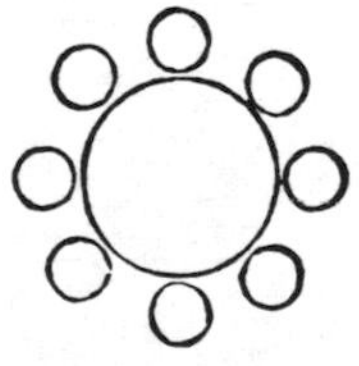

Owadzima.

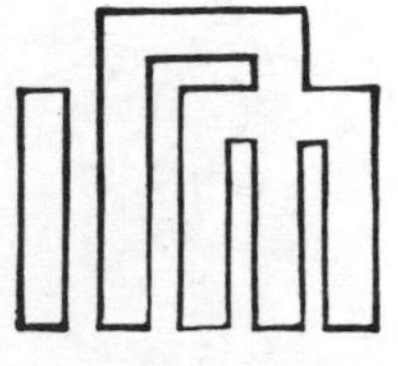

Akita.

Prince of Hizen.

Daïmios.

Daïmios.

Mark	Provinces and Principal Factories.
	GOKINAI.
山城	1. Yamasiro. *Miaco, or the principality of Kiota, is in this province. Awata, Uji, Kiyomidsu.*
大和	2. Yamato. *Koriyama.*
河内	3. Kawatsi or Kawaji. *Hiogo, Awadji.*
和泉	4. Idsoumi. *Fushimi.*
攝津	5. Setsou or Sidzu. *Oosaka, Saki.*
	TOKAIDO.
伊賀	1. Iga.
伊勢	2. Isé or Isyé. *Yokkaich*
志摩	3. Sima.
尾張	4. Owari. *Okasaki, Seto, Shinoyama, Inaki-mura.*
參河	5. Mikawa.
遠江	6. Tootomi (Tohôdomi). *Shitoro-mura.*
駿河	7. Sourouga.
甲斐	8. Kahi or Kii. *Wagayama.*
伊豆	9. Idsou. *Simoda.*
相模	10. Sangami. *Fusiyama mons.*
武藏	11. Mousasi. *Yedo, Tokio, Yokohama, Asakusa, Imado, Kemume-mura.*

Provinces and Principal Factories.	
安房	12. Awa.
上総	13. Kadsousa.
下総	14. Simôsa.
常陸	15. Hitatsi.
TOSANDO.	
近江	1. Oomi. *Zeze, Kimpozan.*
美濃	2. Mino.
飛騨	3. Hida or Fida.
信濃	4. Sinano.

Provinces and Principal Factories.	
上野	5. Kôtsouké.
下野	6. Simotsouké.
武蔵	7. Moutsu.
出羽	8. Déwa.
FOKOUROKOUDO.	
若狭	1. Wakasa.
越前	2. Yetsizen.
加賀	3. Kanga. *Kutani, Ohimachi.*
能登	4. Noto.

	Provinces and Principal Factories.
越中	5. Yetsisiou.
越後	6. Yetsigo.
佐渡	7. Sado (Island).

SANINDO.

丹波	1. Tanba.
丹後	2. Tango.
但馬	3. Tatsima.
因幡	4. Imaba.
伯耆	5. Foki or Hooki.

	Provinces and Principal Factories.
出雲	6. Idsoumo. *Madsuye, Sagai.*
石見	7. Iwami or Iwaki. *Nagamuru, Soma.*
隠岐	8. Oki (Island).

SANYODO.

播磨	1. Arima or Halima. *Himeji.*
美作	2. Mimasaka.
備中	3. Bitsiou.
備前	4. Bizen. *Imbe.*
備後	5. Bingo.

Provinces and Principal Factories.	
安藝	6. Aki.
周防	7. Souwo.
長門	8. Nagato. *Hagi, Madsu, Toyoura-yama.*
NANKAIDO.	
	1. Awadsi or Awaji (Island).
	2. Awa.
	3. Sanouki.
	4. Iyo.
	5. Tosa.

Provinces and Principal Factories.	
	1. Bouzen or Budsen.
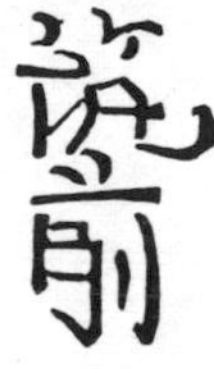	2. Tsikousen. *Sobaramura, Yanagawa.*
	3. Tsikoungo.
	4. Boungo.
	5. Hizen; in the Island of Kin-Siu. *Imali, Matsoura, Arita, Nagasaki, Desima, Karatsu, Okawaji, Mikawaji.*
	6. Figo or Higo.
	7. Fiouga or Hiouga.

Provinces and Principal Factories.		Provinces and Principal Factories.	
大隅	8. Ohosoumi or Osumi. *Chiusa.*	壹岐	10. Iki (Island).
薩摩 B	9. Satsuma. *Nawa-shiro-gawa.*	對馬	11. Tsousima (Island).

NOTE.

The usual terminations, following the Chinese or Japanese marks of dynasties, provinces, or factories, as well as those of potters, are here given :—

 *dzo* or *tzo*, "maker."

 *sei*, "made," same as Chinese *tchi*.

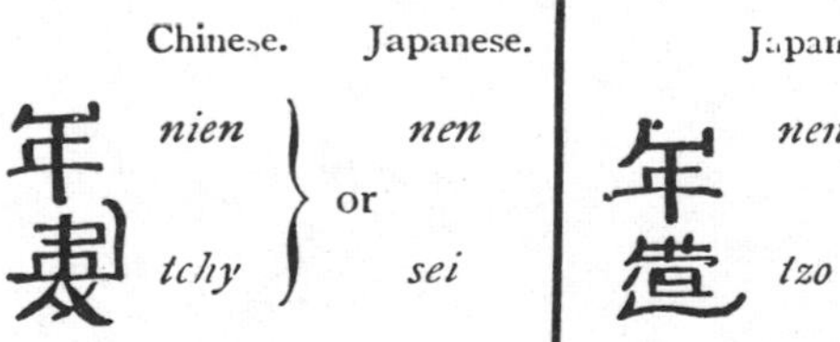

"made in the period."

JAPANESE SEXAGENARY CYCLE, OF 60 YEARS.

TEN SERIES CYCLE. SIGNS OF THE ELEMENTS.

由	1. *Ki nó ye* . . .	*Ki*, Wood	木
乙	2. *Ki nó ye* . . .		
丙	3. *Fi nó ye* . . .	*Fi*, Fire	火
丁	4. *Fi nó to* . . .		
戊	5. *Tsütsi nó ye* . . .	*Tsützi*, Earth . . .	土
己	6. *Tsütsi nó to* . . .		
庚	7. *Kane nó ye* . . .	*Kane*, Metal . . .	金
辛	8. *Kane nó ye* . . .		
壬	9. *Midzü nó ye* . . .	*Midzü*, Water . . .	木
癸	10. *Midzü nó to* . . .		

TWELVE SERIES CYCLE. SIGNS OF THE ZODIAC.

子	1. *Ne* . . .	Mouse.	午	7. *M'ma* . .	Horse.
丑	2. *Usi* . . .	Bull.	未	8. *Fitsúzi* . .	Goat.
寅	3. *Tora* . . .	Tiger.	申	9. *Saru* . . .	Ape.
卯	4. *U* . . .	Hare.	酉	10. *Tori* . . .	Cock.
辰	5. *Tat'* . . .	Dragon.	戌	11. *Inü* . . .	Hound.
巳	6. *Mi* . . .	Serpent.	亥	12. *I* . . .	Swine.

SYNOPSIS OF THE SEXAGENARY CYCLE.

	甲	乙	丙	丁	戊	己	庚	辛	壬	癸
子	1		13		25		37		49	
丑		2		14		26		38		50
寅	51		3		15		27		39	
卯		52		4		16		28		40
辰	41		53		5		17		29	
巳		42		54		6		18		30
午	31		43		55		7		19	
未		32		44		56		8		20
申	21		33		45		57		9	
酉		22		34		46		58		10
戌	11		23		35		47		59	
亥		12		24		36		48		60

The cycle of ten series is derived from the five elements—wood, fire, earth, metal, and water—which, each taken double, are distinguished as masculine and feminine, or, after the Japanese conception, as the elder and younger brother 兄エ *ye*, and 弟ト *to*.

The cycle of twelve series has relation to the division of the zodiac into twelve equal parts, and bears the name of the Chinese zodiac, for which Japanese names of animals are used, as above.

If both series are let proceed side by side till both are run out, then the sixty series cycle is obtained, of which the first year is called 甲子年, *Kíno ye ne no tosi*, and the sixtieth, 癸亥年, *Mĭdzŭ nó to i no tosi*.

The first year of which may thus be explained: *kíno* (wood), *ye* (elder), *ne* (mouse), *no tosi* (of the year). The last or sixtieth: *mĭdzŭ nó* (water), *to* (younger), *I* (swine), *no tosi* (of the year;—*no*, "of," the genitive termination).

		A.D.			A.D.
建德	*Ken-tok*	1370.	永正	*Yei-show*	1504.
文中	*Bun-tin*	1372.	大永	*Dai-jei*	1521.
天授	*Ten-du*	1375.	享祿	*Kiyo-rok*	1528.
弘和	*Ko-wa*	1380.	天永	*Di-yei*	1532.
元中	*Gen-tin*	1380.	弘治	*Ko-dsi*	1555.
明德四	*Mei-tok the IV.*	1393.	永祿	*Yei-rok*	1558.
應永	*O-yei*	1394.	元龜	*Gen-ki*	1570.
正長	*Show-tiyo*	1428.	天正	*Ten-show*	1573.
永享	*Yei-kiyo*	1429.	文祿	*Bun-rok*	1592.
嘉吉	*Ka-kitsu*	1441.	慶長	*Kei-chiyo*	1596.
文安	*Bun-an*	1444.	元和	*Gen-wa*	1615.
宝德	*Ko-tok*	1449.	寛永	*Kwan-jei*	1624.
享德	*Kiyo-tok*	1452.	正保	*Show-ho*	1644.
康正	*Ko-show*	1455.	慶安	*Kei-an*	1648.
長祿	*Chiyo-rok*	1457.	承應	*Show-o*	1652.
寛正	*Kwan-show*	1460.	明曆	*Mei-reki*	1655.
文正	*Bun-show*	1466.	萬治	*Man-dsi*	1658.
應仁	*O-nin*	1467.	寛文	*Kwan-bun*	1661.
文明	*Bun-mei*	1469.	延寶	*Yem-pō*	1673.
長享	*Tiyo-kiyo*	1487.	天和	*Ten-wa*	1681.
延德	*En-tok*	1489.	貞享	*Tei-kiyo*	1684.
明應	*Mei-o*	1492.	元祿	*Gen-rok*	1688.
文龜	*Bun-ki*	1501.	寶永	*Ho-yei*	1704.

		A.D.			A.D.
正德	*Show-tok* . .	1711.	文化	*Bun-kwa* . .	1804.
享保	*Kiyo-ho* . .	1717.	文政	*Bun-sei* . .	1818.
元文	*Gen-bun* . .	1736.	天保	*Ten-foo* . .	1830.
寛保	*Kwan-pō* . .	1741.	弘化	*Koo-kwa* . .	1844.
延享	*Yen-kiyo* . .	1744.	嘉永	*Ka-yei* . .	1848.
寛延	*Kwan-yen* . .	1748.	安政	*An-sei* . .	1854.
寶暦	*Ho-reki* . .	1751.	萬延	*Man-en* . .	1860.
明和	*Mei-wa* . .	1764.	文久	*Bun-kiu* . .	1861.
安永	*An-jei* . .	1772.	元治	*Gen-dzi* . .	1864.
天明	*Ten-mei* . .	1781.	慶應	*Kei-oo* . .	1865.
寛政	*Kwan-sei* . .	1789.	明治	*Mei-ji*, 1868 to present time.	
享和	*Kiyo-wa* . .	1801.			

EXAMPLES OF DATES.

元龜年製	*Gen-ki nen-sei.* A.D. 1570.	延寶年製	*Yem-po nen-sei.* A.D. 1673 to 1681.
天正柒歲	*Ten-show.* A.D. 1579.	文化年製	*Bun-kua nen-sei.* A.D. 1804 to 1818.
承應貳歲	*Show-o.* A.D. 1653.	明治年陶園製	*Mei-ji-nen To-yen-sei.* A.D. 1868.
羕應貳歲	*Eul-soui Yang-ing.* A.D. 1653.		END OF NENGOOS.

One	1	一	*Itsi.*
Two	2	二	*Ni.*
Three	3	三	*San.*
Four	4	四	*Si.*
Five	5	五	*Go.*
Six	6	六	*Roku.*
Seven	7	七	*Sitsi.*
Eight	8	八	*Fatsi.*
Nine	9	九	*Kew.*
Ten	10	十	*Ziyu.*
Hundred	100	百	*Fiyak.*
Thousand	1000	千	*Sen.*
Ten thousand . .	10,000	萬	*Man* or *Ban.*
Eleven	11	十一	The mark for 1 is placed below that for 10.
Twenty-one . .	21	二十一	To denote 20, 30, &c., the marks are placed above 10.
Fifty-one	51	五十一	
Sixty	60	六十	The symbol for 6 placed above 10.
Two hundred . .	200	二百	The symbol for 2 placed above 100, and so on.

KIOTO (Province).
Formerly MIACO.

京都

Fushimi. A copy of style.
Koyemon, potter.

Asahi, in Uji.

1730.

1750.

Kiyomidsu. Ken-Zan, potter.

1840.

Raku. Zengoro, potter, 1810.

Kiyomidsu.
Dohachi, potter, 1875.

Kiyomidsu. Sei-fu, potter, 1875.

Nin-sei, potter at Monomura, 1690.

Kanzan, potter of Kioto, 1860.

Kanzan, potter, 1870.

Tai-zan, potter, 1870.

Itsi-gaya. Tai-zan, potter, 1870.

Tai-zan, potter.

Den-ko, potter, 1870.

Awata ware (*Yaki*).

Awata, 1800.
Cheou, keih, fuh, che, luh.
"The Five Blessings."

YAMATO or AMATO (Province).

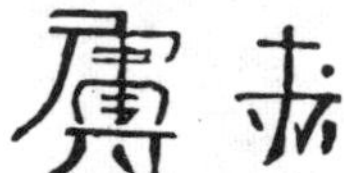

Agahada, at *Koriyama*, 1650.

Aga-hada ("Raw flesh"), 1840.

Agahada. By Tan-sat-su-do, 1650.

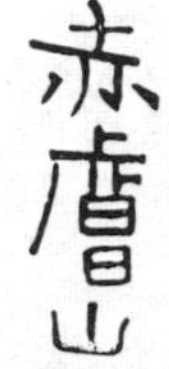

Agahada. Boku-haku, potter.

IDSUMI (Province).

Minatō. Senshui-Sagai-moto.
Kichi-ye-mon, potter, 18th Century.

SETSOU (Province).

Raku ware. ***Kissu-ko***, potter, 1860.

ISÉ or ISYÉ (Province).

Isé ware, 1580. *Fou-kou*, "happiness."

Isé Banko ware.

1870.

Isé Banko ware. Inscription, and name in oval.

Isé Banko marks, 1875.

1875.

OWARI (Province).

Inu-yama ware.

Ho-raku (name of fabric), 1820.

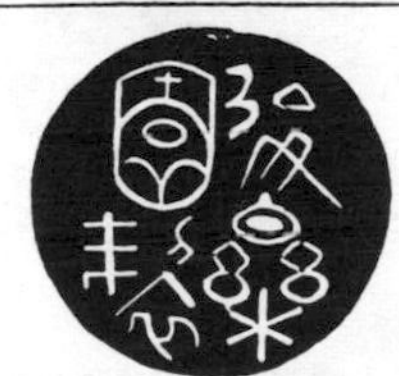

Go-raku (name of fabric), 1820.

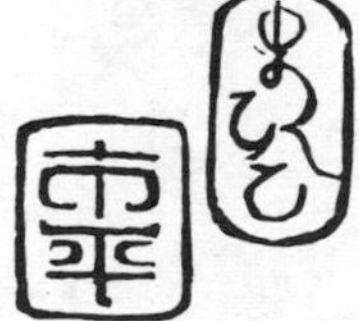

Go-raku and potter's name.

Sedo ware or *Seto*, 1764.

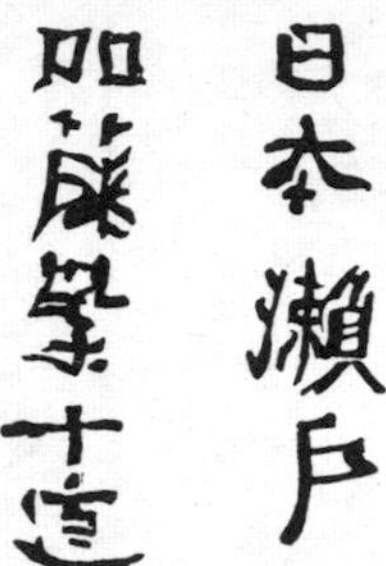

Sometsuke ware, made at Sedo, 1800.

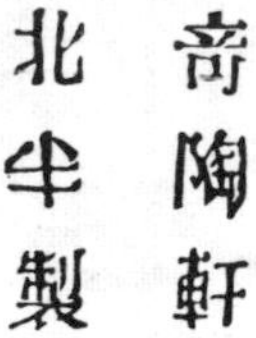

奇陶軒 北半製

Kito-Ken. Hoku-han-sei.

Nipon-Sedo-Kawamotō-Masukichi-tzo, 1874.

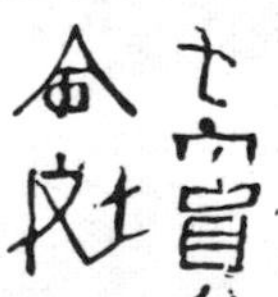

Nagoya ware, by Shippo Kuwaisha, 1876.

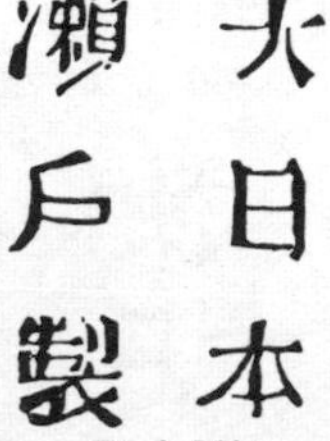

大日本 瀬戸製

Sedo ware. *Dai-Nipon-Sedo-sei.*

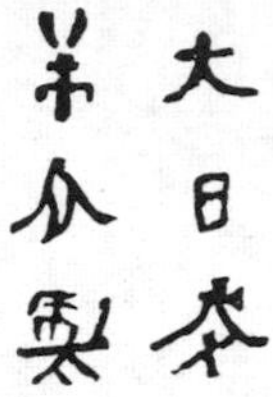

大日本 半介製

Sedo ware, 1876.

Dai-Nipon-Hansuke-sei.

KII OR KAYEI (PROVINCE).

Kishiu ware, 1800.

Kai-raku-yen-sei.

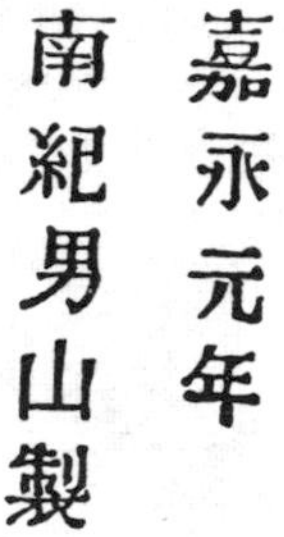

嘉永元年 南紀男山製

Kishiu ware, 1848.

Ka-yei guan-yen Nanki Otoko yama.

Kishiu ware, 1828.

Nanki Otoko-yama.

Cheou, "Long life." Ornamental form on various wares.

Iga ware, made at Kimpozan.

MOUSASI (PROVINCE).

東京

Tokio, now called Yedo.

萬古

Yedo Banko ware, 1750.

壽

Yedo Banko ware, 1750.

Raku ware.

Kozawa Benshi, potter, 1875.

眞葛窯香山造

Ma-kuzu-yo-Kozan-tzo, 1875.

Tokio ware. Hiyochiyen, potter, 1875.

Mino ware. Kado Gosuke, potter, 1875.

KANGA OR KAGA (PROVINCE)

Kanga Kutani, 1867.

Kanga Kutani, 1867.

Kutani-tzo, 1867.

Kutani mark, 1875.

Fou-kou. "Happiness," 1620.

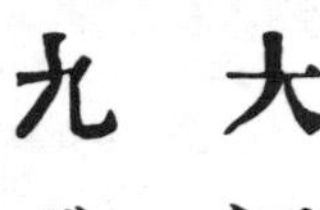

Dai Nipon Kutani-tzo, 1870.

Kutani, and potter's mark, 1870.

Kutani. Uchiumi, potter, 1875.

Kutani. Tou-zan, potter, 1860.

Kutani. Inscription begins at top and reads to the left, 1875.

Ohi Machi. *Raku* ware, 1800.

Ohi Machi. *Raku* ware, 1800.

IDSUMO (PROVINCE).

Fushina ware. Made at Mansuye, 1820.

Fushina ware, 1830.

Fushina. Kano Itsu-sen-in, 1840.

Fushina, 1750.

IWAMI (Province).

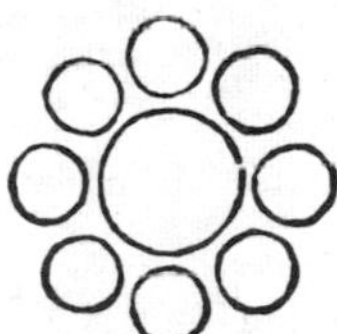

Soma ware. Badge of the Prince.

Soma ware, 1840.

Fuh, "Happiness" on *Soma*, &c., 1840.

Soma. Mark of Yen-Zan.

Soma. Mark of Kane-Shige.

HARIMA (Province)

Tozan. Made at Himeji, 1820.

Tozan ware, 1820.

A stamp unknown, 1760.

Hirado ware. Made at Mikawaji, 1770.

Bizen, 1840.

AWAJI (Island).

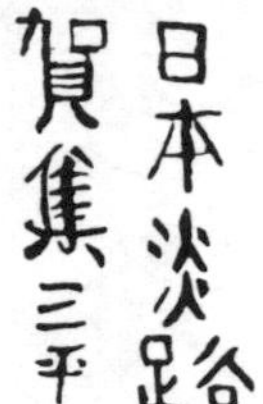

Nipon Awaji Kashiu Sanpei, 1875.

HIZEN (Province).

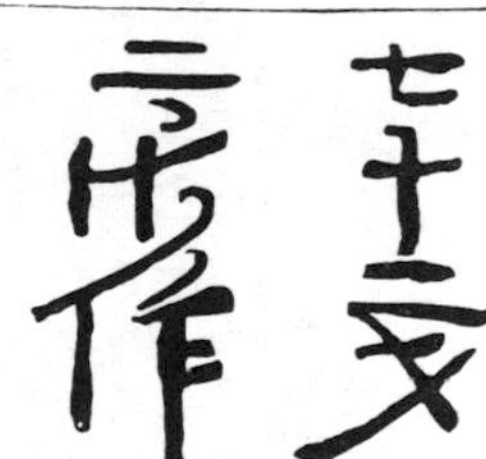

Jiraku ware, at Karatsu, 1800.

Mikawaji, near Arita, 1760.

Okawaji, near Arita.

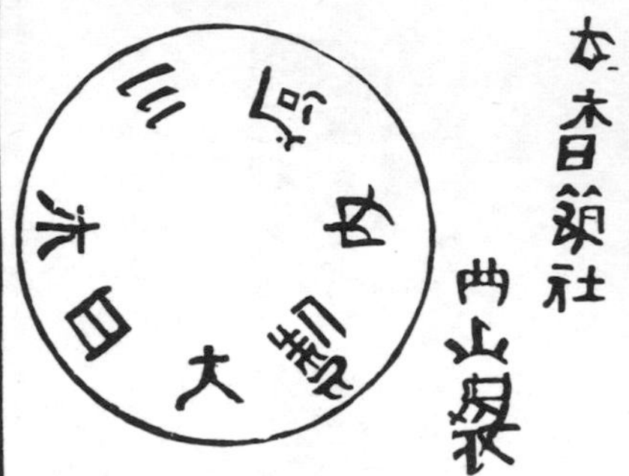

Made at *Mikawaji*. The inscription begins at bottom, reading left. 1875.

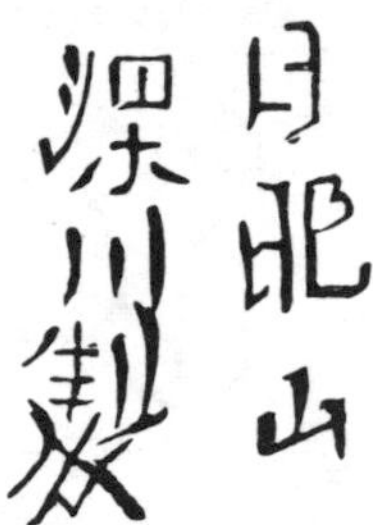

Okawaji. Imari ware, 1875.

Imari in Hizen.

Zo-shun ware.

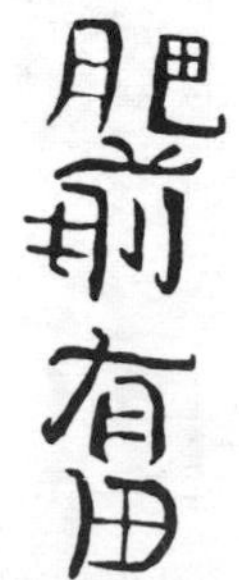

Imari in Arita.

Imari ware, made at *Arita*, 1800.

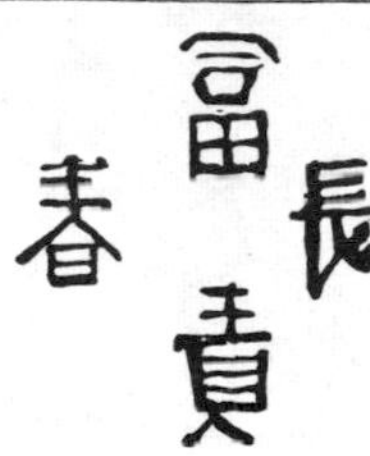

Arita. *Fuh-kouei-chang-chun*, "The Five Blessings," 1810.

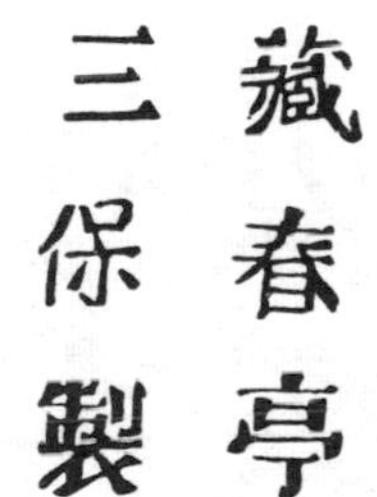

Zôshun-tei-Sampo-sei, 1830.

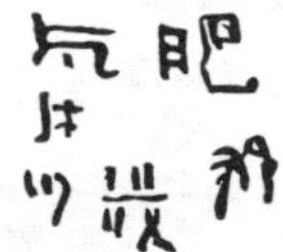

Arita ware (*Imari*). Fukagawa, potter.

Arita ware, made by S. Fukami, 1875.

Imari, by S. Fukami, 1875.

Kisa. Koransha mark of S. Fukami, 1875.

Dai Nipon Hizen.

Mark of Y. Fukagawa of Arita, 1875, on the above.

ITALY.

FLORENCE, 1580. The cathedral.

FLORENCE. XVI Century.
Arms of the Medici.

FLORENCE. XVI Century.
A lion's paw holding a tablet.

FLORENCE.

DOCCIA. Established 1735.

DOCCIA. Fanciullacci.

GINORI.

DOCCIA. XVIII Century.

DOCCIA. XVIII Century.

CAPO DI MONTE.
Established 1736, ceased 1821.

CAPO DI MONTE. Circa 1759.
N crowned for Naples.

CAPO DI MONTE. Circa 1780.
Rex Ferdinandus.

Apiello

CAPO DI MONTE. Painter.

B.G.

NAPLES. Giustiniani.

MILAN. J. Richard. XIX Century.

G.A.F.F.

Treviso.

TREVISO.

Giuseppe Andrea Fontebasso, Fratelli.

F. F.

Treviso. 1799

TREVISO. Fratelli Fontebasso.

TURIN (Vineuf). Established 1770.

Doctor Gioanetti.

V.F

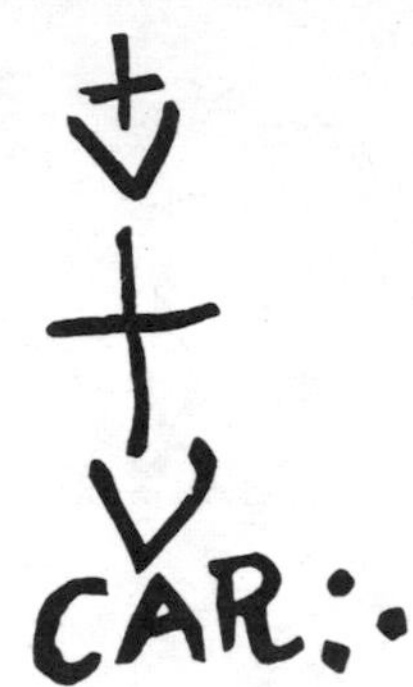

TURIN (Vineuf).

VICENZA.

1765

Venezia

Fab^{a}. Geminiano

COZZI

VENICE.

V^{a}

VENICE. Established circa 1720.

C. P.

N. 3.

VENICE.
Initials with prices underneath.

Ven^a A.G. 1726.

VENICE, an early mark.

A. G.
*

A E.W.
I.W

VENICE. Unknown marks.

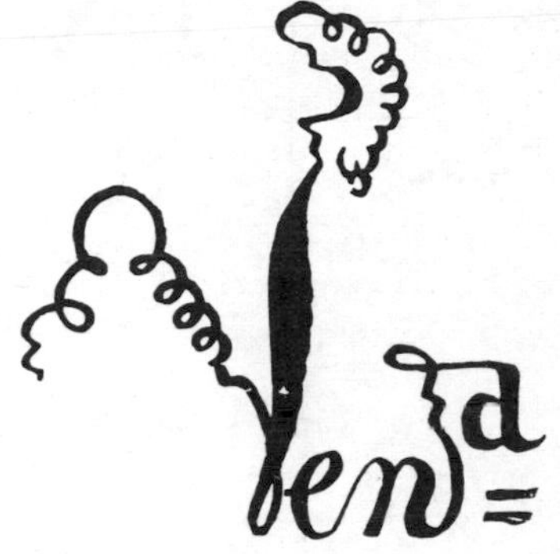

VENICE. Marks of the Vezzi period.
Established 1723, ceased circa 1750.

Lodovico Ortolani Veneto
dipinse nella Fabrica di
Porcelana, in Venetia

VENICE. Ortolani, circa 1740.

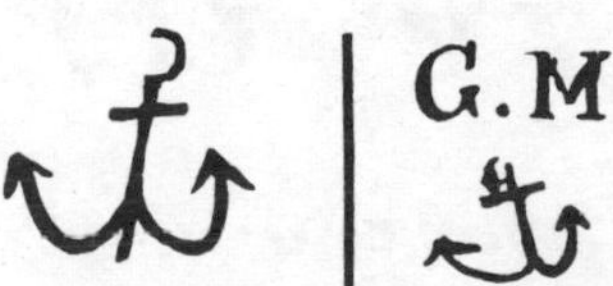

Cozzi period. Giovanni Marconi.

VENICE. Marks of the Cozzi period. Established 1765.

NOVE. Established 1752. Giovanni Battista Antonibon.

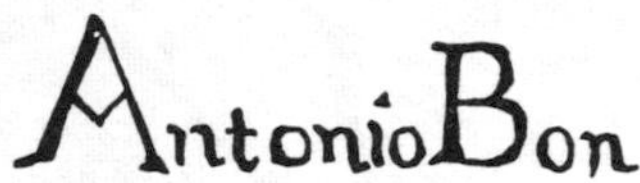

NOVE. Antonibon.

ue
No:
G·B·A·B:

NOVE. Giovanni Battista, Antonio Bon or Antonibon.

Gio.ni Marconi pinx.t

NOVE. Marconi, painter.

NOVE. XVIII Century.

Nove
Nove

Nove
*

NOVE
*

Fabbrica Baroni
Nove.

NOVE. Baroni period, 1802–1825.

Nove. Baroni.

Nove. XVIII Century.

ESTE + 1783 +

Este, near Padua. XVIII Century.

D·B

ESTE

GF

Este.

SPAIN.

Gerona.

Note.—Probably a Spanish coat-of-arms on Oriental porcelain.

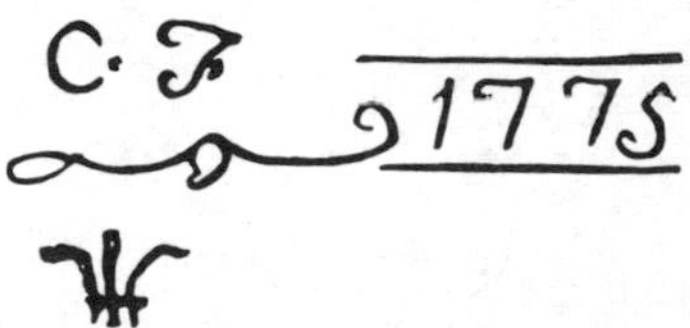

Madrid. Cayetano fecit.

Madrid (Buen Retiro).
Established 1760, ceased 1808.

Madrid. Salvador Nofri.

MADRID. Ochogravia?

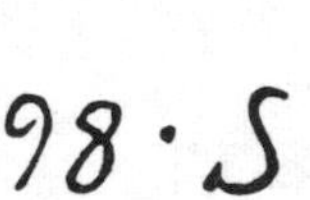

MADRID. Sorrentini?

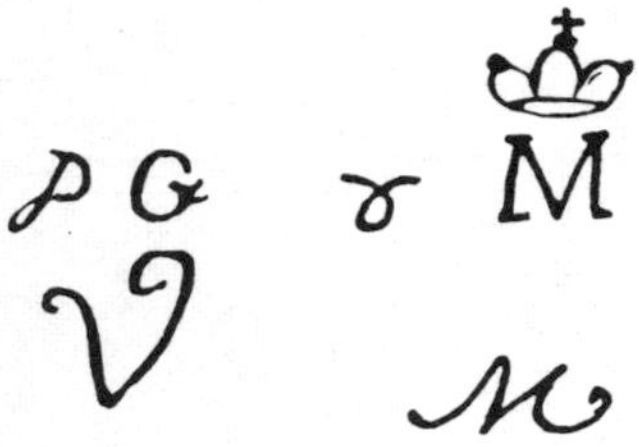

MADRID. Pedro Georgi?

MADRID. Unknown.

MADRID. Charles III.

R. F. Đ. PORCELANA

Đ. S. M. C.

MADRID. On imitation Wedgwood.

MADRID. XVIII Century

MADRID. XVIII Century.

MADRID (Buen Retiro).
Established 1763, ceased 1808.

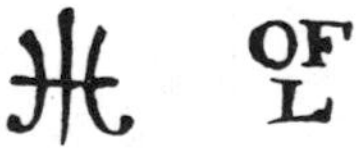

MADRID.

OPORTO. Vista Allegre. Established about 1790.

GERMANY.

DRESDEN (Meissen).
Augustus Rex, 1709–1726. For the King's use.

DRESDEN. Wand of Æsculapius.
Established c. 1712. Porcelain for sale, 1715 to 1720.

DRESDEN.
Comtesse de Cosel's service.

DRESDEN, 1716 to 1720.

DRESDEN.
Böttger's marks.

DRESDEN.
Böttger's marks.

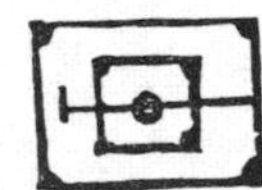

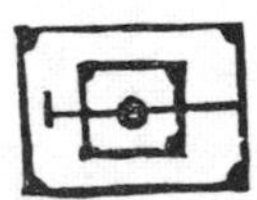

DRESDEN, about 1720.

DRESDEN. Early marks, c. 1730.

DRESDEN. King's period, 1770.

DRESDEN, about 1796. One or more stars denote the Marcolini period.

B.P.T.
Dresden.17.39.

K.H.C.W.

DRESDEN (Meissen).

M.P.M.

DRESDEN.

DRESDEN (Meissen).

NOTE.—One bar across the swords on white china signifies *perfect* and *for sale.*
One or two above or below signifies *defective.*
Two to four across on services, more or less *defective.*

Königliche Porzellan Manufactur.

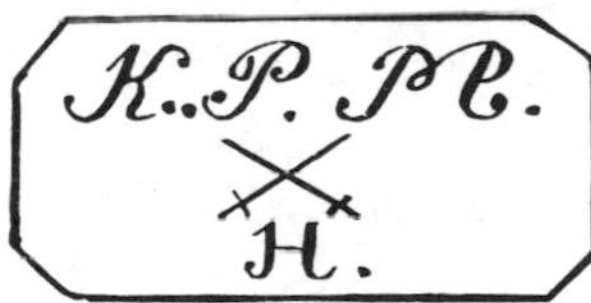

C.F. Kühnel
35 Jahr in Dienst
57 Jahr alt
1776

C.F Herold
invt; et fecit, a meissē
1750. d 12 Sept:

DRESDEN (Meissen).

Alex Tromery
a Berlin

DRESDEN.

L T.

W
AB 1726

G.L
1728
30 Dec:

K.H.C.W.

DRESDEN.

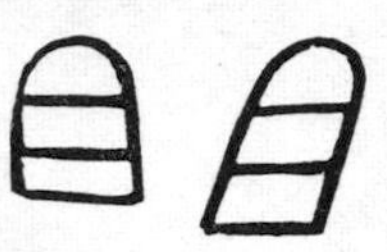

VIENNA.
Established 1718, ceased 1864.

Joseph Nigg.

LAMPRECHT.

Perger.

Furstler.

VARSANNI.

J. Wech.

K. Herr.

VIENNA. Artists.

S

SCHLAKENWALD. Established 1800.

ELBOGEN.
Established 1815. Haidinger.

NOWOTNY.

A.N.

ALTENROLHAU. Nowotny.

HEREND.

Herend.

HEREND. Arms of Hungary.
XVIII Century.

MF

HEREND. Morice Fischer.

C.F.

PIRKENHAMMER. Christian Fischer.

F&R

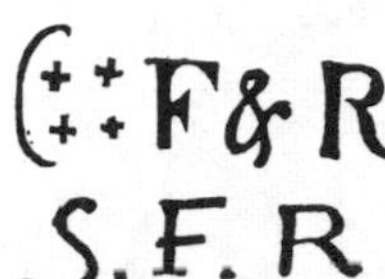

PIRKENHAMMER.
Fischer and Reichambach.

PRAGUE. Kriegel and Co.

BERLIN. Wegeley. Established 1751.

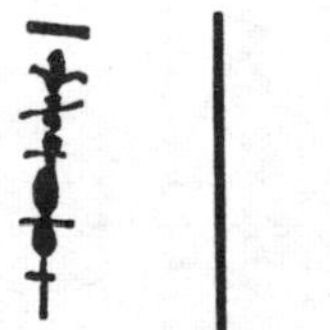

BERLIN. Sceptre, 1761.

BERLIN. Used c. 1830.

WE

BERLIN. Various marks.

CHARLOTTENBURG. Established 1760.

B. P. M.

BERLIN.

MOABIT near BERLIN.
Established 1835.

HÖCHST. Established by Gelz, 1720.

FRANKENTHAL.
Crest used from 1755 to 1761.

FRANKENTHAL. J. A. Hannong.

FRANKENTHAL.
Mark of Carl Theodor, 1761.

FRANKENTHAL.

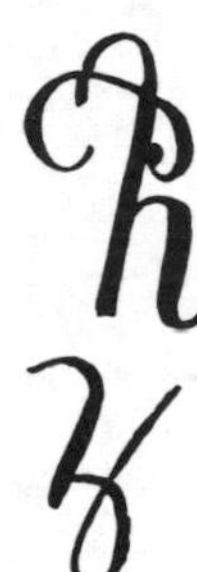

FRANKENTHAL. Hannong.

IHI

FRANKENTHAL.

F.B

GREINSTADT. Bartolo.

NYMPHENBURG. Established 1758.
Arms of Bavaria.

NYMPHENBURG.

I.A.H
1778
D. 17. 8bl

C. H. Silbertamer.
1771.

J. Willand Jne

G. C. LINDEMAN
Pinxit.

NYMPHENBURG. Painters.

NYMPHENBURG.

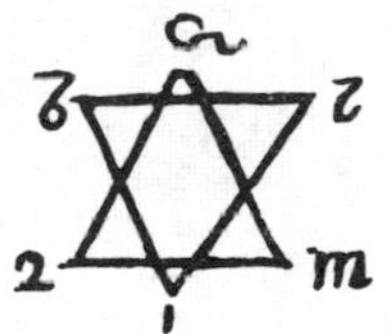

NYMPHENBURG. Masonic.

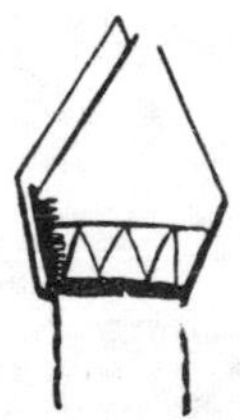

WURTZBURG. XVIII Century.

Bäyreith
1744

Baijreuth
Fec Jucht

BAYREUTH. XVIII Century.

ANSPACH (BAVARIA).
Established 1718.

ANSPACH. XVIII Century.

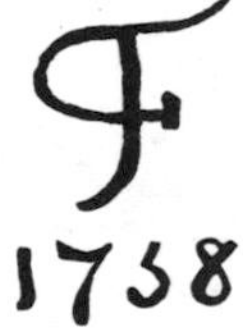

FURSTENBURG. Established 1750.

FURSTENBURG. Established 1763.

LUDWIGSBURG.

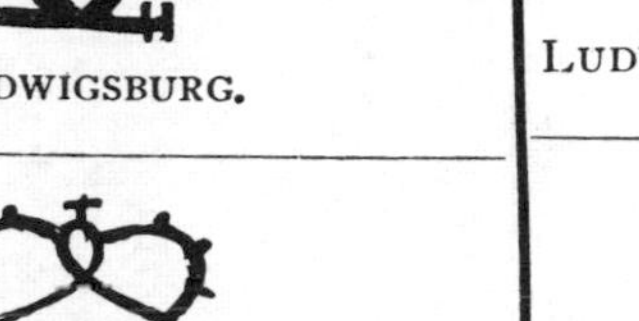

LUDWIGSBURG or KRONENBURG.
Established by Ringler, 1758.

LUDWIGSBURG, before 1806.

LUDWIGSBURG. Arms of Wurtemburg.

LUDWIGSBURG.
Used from 1806 to 1818.

LUDWIGSBURG, 1806 to 1818.

LUDWIGSBURG, from 1818.

HILDESHEIM. Established 1760.

FULDA. Established 1763.

FULDA, ceased 1780.

HESSE-DARMSTADT. Estab[d.] 1756.

VC and GV.

VOLKSTEDT.
Established 1762, by Greiner.

VOLKSTEDT.

RUDOLSTADT. Established 1762.

RUDOLSTADT.
A hay-fork. Arms of Schwartzbourg.

R. g.

REGENSBURG or RATISBON.

R—n

RAUENSTEIN. Established 1760.

WALLENDORF. Established 1762.

GROSBREITENBACH. Estab[d]. 1770.

GROSBREITENBACH, 1770.

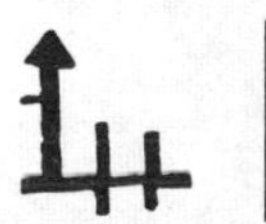

THURINGIA. Uncertain.

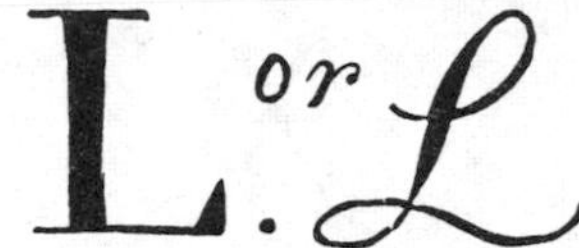

LIMBACH. Established c. 1761, by Gotthelf Greiner.

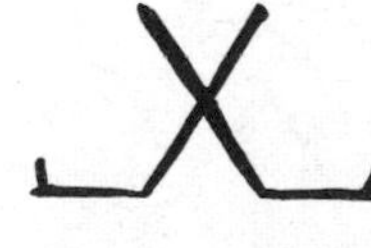

LIMBACH, 1761.

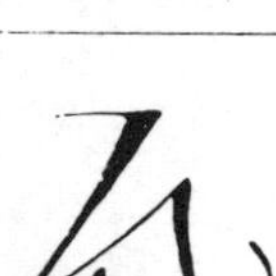

LIMBACH, 1761.

GERA. Established about 1780.

Gotha

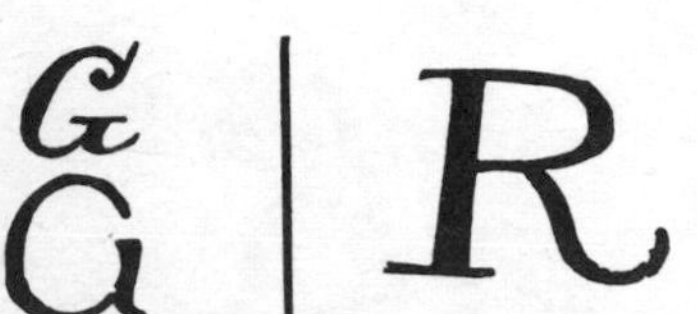

GOTHA. Various marks.

GOTHA.
Established 1780. Rothenberg.

HALDENSTEBEN. Nathusius.

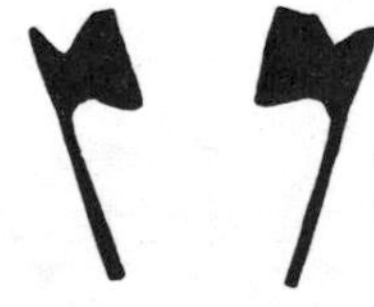

BADEN. Established 1753, by the Widow Sperl, ceased 1778.

SWITZERLAND.

Gide 1789.

NYON. Established about 1780.

NYON, 1780-1790, Genese.

ZURICH. Established 1759.

HOLLAND. BELGIUM.

WEESP. Established 1764.

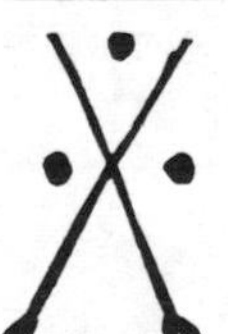

WEESP. XVIII Century.

WEESP. XVIII Century.

LM
W

WEESP or LOOSDRECHT.

Mo L

M*.oL

M:oL

LOOSDRECHT.
Established 1772, by Rev. De Mol and others. Manufactur oude Loosdrecht.

A: Lafond & Comp
à Amsterdam

AMSTERDAM. Circa 1810.

AMSTERDAM. XVIII Century.

Amstel.

OUDE AMSTEL. Established 1782.

AMSTEL. A. Dareuber, Director. Ceased about 1800.

:Amstel

NIEWER AMSTEL, by Dommer & Co.

THE HAGUE.
Established 1775, by Leichner; ceased 1786.

LILLE.

fait par
Lebrun à Lille

LILLE.
Established 1711, by Dorez and Pelissier. These marks are of the period of Leperre Durot, 1784.

TOURNAY.

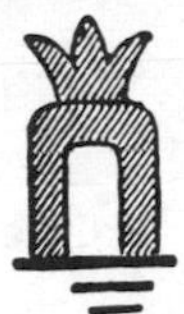

TOURNAY.
Established about 1750, by Peterinck.

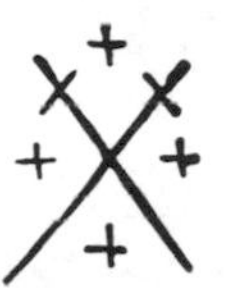

TOURNAY, used about 1760.

To Tʏ

TOURNAY (so ascribed).

.EB.

BRUSSELS. XVIII Century.

Lr Cretté de Bruxelles
rue D'Aremberg 1791.

L C.

BRUSSELS, with initials of L. Cretté.

L.C.

Ebenstein

BRUSSELS, with painter's name.

BRUSSELS. XVIII Century.

B.L.

BL

LUXEMBURG. Boch. Established Sept Fontaines. Circa 1806.

RUSSIA. POLAND.

ST. PETERSBURG. Established 1744.

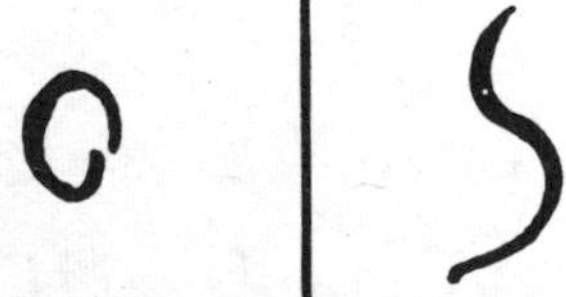

ST. PETERSBURG.

П:К.

ST. PETERSBURG.
Initials of Empress Catherine II., 1762–1796. Paul Korneloffe, maker.

ST. PETERSBURG.
Initial of Emperor Paul, 1706–1801.

St. Petersburg.
Emperor Alexander I., 1801–1825.

St. Petersburg.
Emperor Nicholas, 1825–1855.

St. Petersburg.
Emperor Alexander II., 1855.

ВРАТЬЕВЪ
Корниловыхъ

St. Petersburg.
Brothers Korneloffe, makers.
Established 1827.

St. Petersburg. Korneloffe.

ГАРДНЕРZ

C

Moscow.

Moscow.
Established 1787, by A. Gardner.

ПОПОВЫ

Moscow.
A. Popoffe, established 1830.

ФГ
ГУЛИНА

Moscow.
Gulena, potter. Fabrica Gospedina.

KIEBZ.

13

11

KIEFF. End of XVIII Century.

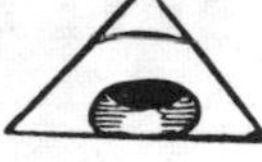

KORZEC.
Established 1803, by Mérault.

BARANOWKA (Poland).

TURKEY.

SWEDEN AND DENMARK.

MARIEBERG.
Estabd. 1770. Frantzen, decorator.

MARIEBERG.
Sten, Director. Circa 1780.

MB

MARIEBERG, 1770–1789.

MARIEBERG. Ceased 1789.

COPENHAGEN.
Established 1772, by Müller.

COPENHAGEN.

H: Ondriip

Ibid. Painter's name.

COPENHAGEN?

B & G

COPENHAGEN.
Bing and Grondahl, 1850.

GERMANY. Uncertain Marks.

B H. D. fecit

CN	
Y	IK
	HK
	HK
NT	C We Dw 1730
M.	R. B. 1750.
×C-L×	G.B.F. 1783.
	E B

FRANCE.

St. Cloud. Chicanneau.

St. Cloud.
Established 1695, ceased 1773.

S^T. C
T

St. Cloud. Trou, 1730–1762.

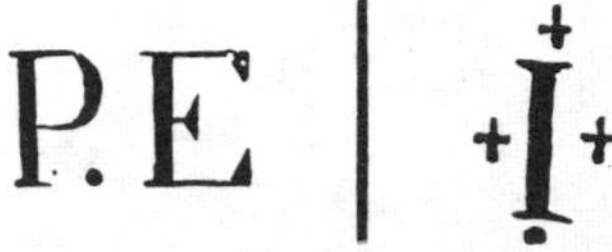

St. Cloud. Successors of Trou.

Chantilly.
Established 1725. Ciquaire Cirou.

Chantilly.

D V

. D.V.

Menecy. Duc de Villeroy. Established 1735, by Barbin, ceased 1773.

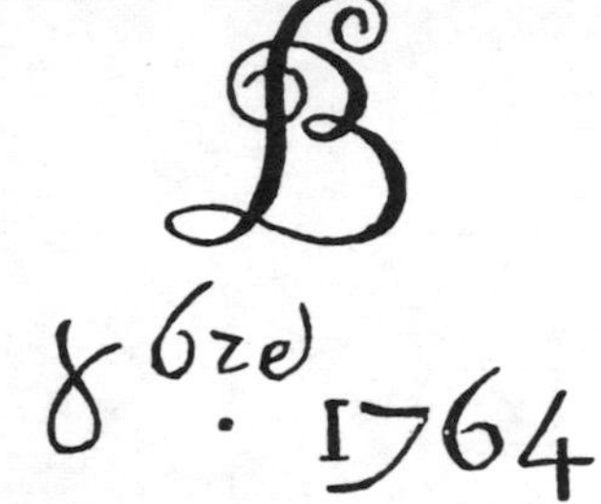

FRANCE. Brancas Lauraguais.
Established 1764.

FRANCE. Brancas Lauraguais.

S.P

SCEAUX.

SCEAUX PENTHIÈVRE.
Established 1750, by Jacques Chapelle.

 AR

ARRAS.
Estab[d.] 1872, by Demoiselles Deleneur.

h et L

VINCENNES. Established 1786.
Hannong and Le Maire.

VINCENNES. Louis Philippe, 1783.

VINCENNES? Dubois.

VINCENNES. Hannong.

BOULOGNE. XIX Century.
M. Haffringue.

ETIOLLES. Established 1768.
Monnier, manufacturer.

ETIOLLES. Pellevé.

BR

OR

B la R

BOURG LA REINE.
Established 1773, by Jacques & Jullien.

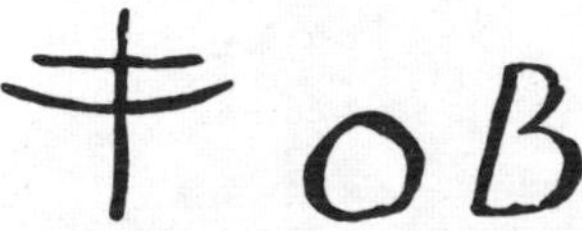

BOURG LA REINE.

CLIGNANCOURT. Established 1775.

CLIGNANCOURT. Deruelle.

CLIGNANCOURT.
Louis Stanislas Xavier. Monsieur,
Comte de Provence.

CLIGNANCOURT. Deruelle.

M

CLIGNANCOURT. Monsieur.

CLIGNANCOURT. Mark of Monsieur, Comte de Provence.

CLIGNANCOURT.

Moitte.

CLIGNANCOURT.
Moitte, successor to Deruelle.

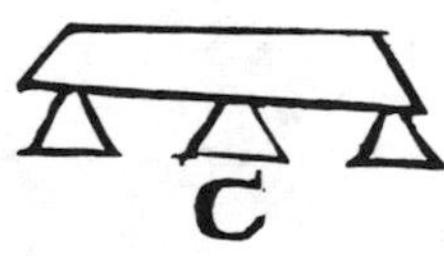

ORLEANS.
Established 1753, by G. Daraubert.

ORLEANS.

orléans

ORLEANS.
Bénoist Le Brun, 1808-1811.

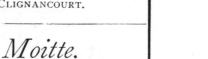

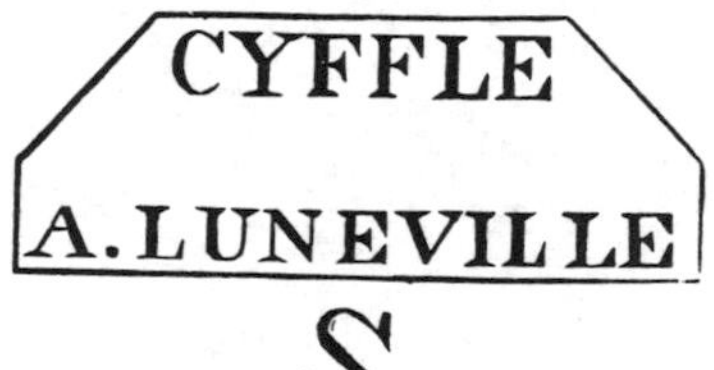

TERRE DE LORRAINE
leopold

LUNEVILLE. Established 1769. Cyfflé.

NIDERVILLER.

NIDERVILLER.
Established 1760, by Baron de Beyerlet.

NIDERVILLER. Count Custine, 1792.

NIDERVILLER.

NIDERVILLER.

NIDERVILLER.
Lanfray. Succeeded 1802 to 1827.

MONTREUIL.

BOISSETTE.
Established 1777, by Vermonet.

VAUX. Established 1770, by Hannong.

La Seinie. Established 1774, by the Comte de la Seinie.

CAEN

Caen. Established 1798, ceased 1808.

Le françois
à
Caen.

Caen. A recent potter.

G
BAYEUX

Bayeux. Established 1810, by Langlois, afterwards M. Gosse.

Bordeaux. Veillard.

Valenciennes. Established 1785. Fauquez and Lamoninary.

Chatillon (Seine). Circa 1775.

St. Amand.
Established 1815, by M. de Bettignies.

CHOISY LE ROY.
Established 1786, by M. Clement.

G R et Cie

LIMOGES. Established 1773. Grellet.

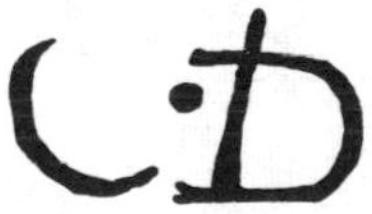

C·D

C:D

LIMOGES. Other marks of early date.
Circa 1773, ceased 1788.

SARGUEMINES. Utzchneider.

SARGUEMINES. Recent mark.

H | PH

B ·*h*·

STRASBOURG, 1752. Hannong.

STRASBOURG, so attributed from the quality of the ware.

STRASBOURG, supposed.

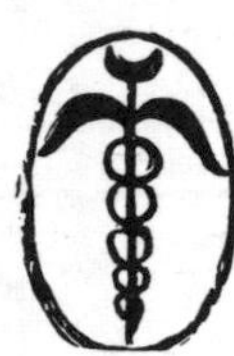

STRASBOURG, supposed.

R | R

MARSEILLE. Established 1766, by J. Gaspard Robert, ceased 1793.

CM

PARIS. Chicanneau & Moreau. Faubourg St. Honoré, 1730.

PARIS. Pont aux Choux, 1784.

PARIS. Pont aux Choux. Louis Philippe, 1786–1793.

PARIS. Pont aux Choux. Outrequin de Montarcy, circa 1786.

C.H

Ch.

PARIS. Faubourg St. Antoine, 1784.
by H. F. Chanou.

L or L

L

PARIS. Rue de Reuilly, 1774,
J. J. Lassia.

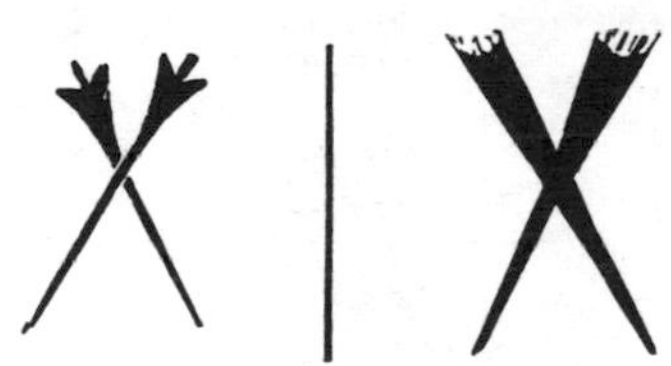

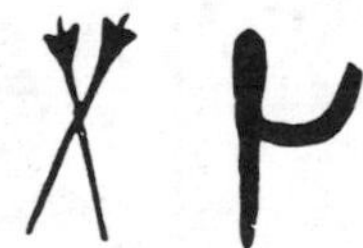

PARIS. "De la Courtille," 1773, by
Russinger & Locré.

manufacture
A. Deltuf

PARIS. "De la Courtille."

Pouyat
&
Ruffinger

P.R.

PARIS. "De la Courtille," 1800.

Monginot
20 Boulevart
des Italiens.

PARIS. Monginot, potter.

MAP

PARIS. Faubourg St. Antoine, 1773.
Morelle à Paris.

H

PARIS. Faubourg St. Lazare, 1773,
by Hannong.

S

PARIS. Rue de la Roquette, 1773,
Souroux, potter.

PARIS. Faubourg St. Antoine, 1773,
Rue de la Roquette. Dubois.

L^{N}. DARTE Rue
Vivienne N.

PARIS. "Gros Caillou," 1773, by Advenir Lamarre.

PARIS. Rue Thiroux. "De la Reine" (Antoinette), 1778, by A. M. Lebeuf.

Housel

PARIS. "De la Reine." Succeeded Lebeuf, 1799.

Gh
Rue Thirou
a Paris.

PARIS. Guy and Housel, 1799.

LEVEILLE
12
Rue THIROUX

PARIS. "De la Reine."

PARIS. "De la Reine." Rue Thiroux.

FLEURY

PARIS. Rue Faub. St. Denis. M. Flamen Fleury.

Flamen
Fleury
Paris.

PARIS.

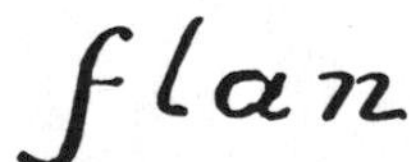

PARIS. Mark unknown.

PARIS. Rue de Clichy.

PARIS. Rue de Bondy, 1780.
"D'Angoulême." Dihl & Guerhard.

PARIS. Rue de Bondy.
"Angoulême."

MANUF RE
M GR le DUC
Angouleme
Paris.

PARIS. Rue de Bondy.

Dihl.

PARIS. Rue de Bondy.

MANUF RE
de M M rs
Guerhard et
Dihl à Paris

PARIS. Rue de Bondy.

REVIL
Rue Neuve
des
Capucines

PARIS. Unknown.

V e M
& C

PARIS. Unknown.

DASTIN.

PARIS. Unknown.

PARIS. Rue Faubourg St. Denis, 1769.
Charles Philippe, Comte d'Artois.

Schoelcher.

PARIS. Boulevard des Italiens.

C. H. PILLIVUYT,
& Cie Paris.

PARIS. FOESCY. MEHUN.

Manufre de Foëscy,
Passage Violet No. 5
R. Poissonnière, à Paris.

PARIS. M. Cottier.

Feuillet

PARIS. Feuillet.

jP.

PARIS.
Belleville, 1790, by Jacob Petit.

R
C·P
1

PARIS. Rue de Crussol, 1789, by Charles Potter.

E.B.

PARIS. Rue de Crussol.

P
CG
Mtu du Pl.
Carousel
à Paris

PARIS. M. Guy, 1775.

T.G.
C.
Paris.

PARIS. Unknown.

NAST

N . . .
à
Paris

PARIS. Rue de Popincourt, 1780.
Le Maire, succeeded by M. Nast.

C. H. MENARD
Paris
72 *Rue de Popincourt.*

PARIS. Gillet & Brianchon, 1857.
Lustred china.

Dagoty
à paris

Manufacture
de S.M.L'Imperatrice.
P.L DAGOTY
à Paris.

PARIS. Boulevard Poissonnière, 1780.

F. M. HONORE

PARIS. Boulevard St. Antoine, 1875.

M^{ture} de MADAME
DUCHESSE D'ANGOULEME
Dagoty E. Honoré,
PARIS.

F. D. HONORÉ
à Paris.

PARIS. Boulevard St. Antoine.

R. F. DAGOTY.

PARIS. Rue St. Honoré.

PARIS. Unknown.

L. Gardie.
a Paris.

PARIS. Unknown.

Lerosey
11 Rue de la paix

PARIS. Modern.

SEVRES MARKS.

FIRST ROYAL EPOCH.

1745 TO 1792.

VINCENNES.
The letter A denotes the year 1753, continued to 1777. (Louis XV.)

SEVRES.
Ornamented LL's. Date 1764.

SEVRES. Date 1754.

SEVRES. Date 1778. (Louis XVI.)
Double letters continued to 1793.

FIRST REPUBLICAN EPOCH.

1792 TO 1804.

R.F
Sevres.

R.F
Sevres.

Sèvres
1792 to 1799.

M N^{le}
Sèvres
1801 to 1804.

FIRST IMPERIAL EPOCH.
1804 TO 1814.

NAPOLEON. 1804 to 1809.

NAPOLEON. 1809 to 1814.

SECOND ROYAL EPOCH.
1814 TO 1848.

Louis XVIII. 1814 to 1823.

Charles X. 1824 to 1829.

Charles X. 1829 and 1830.

Charles X. 1830.

Louis Philippe. 1831 to 1834.

Louis Philippe. 1834-1835.

On services for the Palaces.

Louis Philippe. 1845-1848.

S . 48.

After 1803, this mark in green was used for white porcelain.

SECOND REPUBLICAN EPOCH.
1848 TO 1851.

The S stands for Sevres, and 51 for 1851.

SECOND IMPERIAL EPOCH.
1852 TO 1872.

Napoleon III. From 1852.

This mark used for white pieces; when scratched it denotes issue undecorated.

SEVRES. Examples of 1770 and 1771, with unknown emblems of painters.

CHRONOLOGICAL TABLE OF SIGNS EMPLOYED IN THE ROYAL MANUFACTORY OF SEVRES.

By which the exact date of any piece may be ascertained. It differs from that before given by M. Brongniart in the addition of the letter J for 1762, and the JJ for 1787, which is now altered on the authority of the late M. Riocreux of the Sevres Museum.

A (Vincennes)	1753	P	1768	EE	1782
B (ditto)	1754	Q	*1769	FF	1783
C (ditto)	1755	R	1770	GG	1784
D	1756	S	1771	HH	1785
E	1757	T	1772	II	1786
F	1758	U	1773	JJ	1787
G	1759	V	1774	KK	1788
H	1760	X	1775	LL	1789
I	1761	Y	1776	MM	1790
J	1762	Z	1777	NN	1791
K	1763	AA	1778	OO	1792
L	1764	BB	1779	PP	1793
M	1765	CC	1780	QQ	1794
N	1766	DD	1781	RR	1795
O	1767				

The letters are sometimes small and occasionally placed outside the double LL.

Year IX	1801	T 9	
,, X	1802	X	
,, XI	1803	11	
,, XII	1804	—//—	
,, XIII	1805	↓	
,, XIV	1806	=	

1807		7
1808		8
1809		9
1810		10
1811	(onze)	o.z.
1812	(douze)	d.z.
1813	(treize)	t.z.
1814	(quatorze)	q.z.
1815	(quinze)	q.n.
1816	(seize)	s.z.
1817	(dix sept)	d.s.

From this date the year is expressed by the last two figures only—thus, 18 for 1818, &c.—up to the present time.

* The comet of 1769 furnished the Administration of the time with the idea of transmitting the recollection by their productions. This comet was sometimes substituted for the ordinary mark of the letter Q.

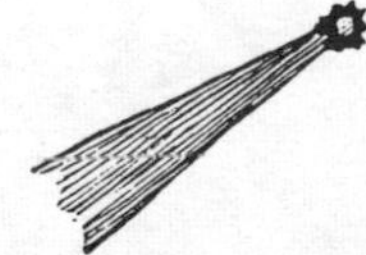

TABLE OF MARKS AND MONOGRAMS

OF

PAINTERS, DECORATORS, AND GILDERS OF THE ROYAL MANUFACTORY OF SEVRES.

1753 TO 1800.

Marks.	*Names of Painters.*	*Subjects.*
	ALONCLE . . .	Birds, flowers, and emblems.
	ANTEAUME . .	Landscapes, and animals.
	ARMAND . . .	Birds, flowers, &c.
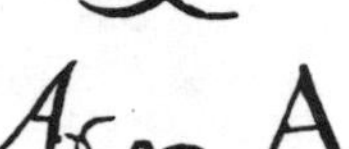	ASSELIN . . .	Portraits, miniatures
 	AUBERT ainé . .	Flowers.
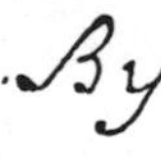	BAILLY . . .	Flowers.
	BAR	Detached bouquets.
	BARBE	Flowers.
	BARDET . . .	Flowers.
	BARRAT . . .	Garlands, bouquets.
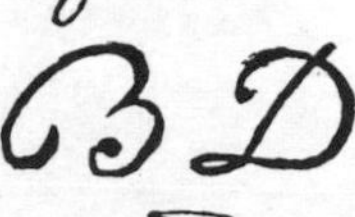	BAUDOUIN . .	Ornaments, friezes.
	BECQUET . . .	Flowers.

Marks.	*Names of Painters.*	*Subjects.*
6.	BERTRAND . .	Detached bouquets.
★	BIENFAIT . . .	Gilding.
·Ṫ	BINET	Detached bouquets.
Sc	BINET, M^dme, *née* Sophie CHANOU.	Garlands, bouquets.
	BOUCHER . . .	Flowers, wreaths.
	BOUCHET . . .	Landscapes, figures, ornaments.
B	BOUCOT . . .	Birds and flowers.
Pb or P.B.	BOUCOT, P. . .	Flowers, birds, and arabesques.
Y·	BOUILLAT . . .	Flowers, landscapes.
R.B.	BOUILLAT, Rachel afterwards M^dme MAQUERET	Detached bouquets.
B.	BOULANGER . .	Detached bouquets.
𝄞	BOULANGER, Jun.	Children, rustic subjects.
Bn.	BULIDON . . .	Detached bouquets.
m.b or MB	BUNEL, M^dme, *née* BUTEUX, Manon	Detached bouquets.

Marks.	*Names of Painters.*	*Subjects.*
	BUTEUX, Sen. .	Cupids, flowers, emblems, &c. *en camaieu.*
9.	BUTEUX, eld. son	Detached bouquets, &c.
	BUTEUX, yr. son .	Pastorals, children, &c.
	CAPELLE . . .	Various friezes.
	CARDIN . . .	Detached bouquets.
5	CARRIER . . .	Flowers.
c.	CASTEL . . .	Landscapes, hunting subjects, birds, &c.
	CATON . . .	Pastorals, children, portraits.
or	CATRICE . . .	Detached bouquets and flowers.
ch.	CHABRY . . .	Miniatures, pastorals
S c	CHANOU, Sophie, afterwards M[dme] BINET	Garlands, bouquets.
c.p.	CHAPUIS, Sen. .	Flowers, birds.
cj or jc.	CHAPUIS, Jun. .	Detached bouquets.
	CHAUVAUX, Sen.	Gilding.

Marks.	*Names of Painters.*	*Subjects.*
j.n.	CHAUVAUX, Jun.	Gilding & bouquets.
	CHEVALIER . .	Flowers, bouquets.
or	CHOISY, DE . .	Flowers, arabesques.
	CHULOT . . .	Emblems, flowers, and arabesques.
c.m. or cm	COMMELIN . .	Garlands, bouquets.
	CORNAILLE . .	Flowers, bouquets.
	COUTURIER . .	Gilding.
	DIEU	Chinese subjects, flowers, gilding.
k or K.	DODIN	Figures, subjects, portraits.
DR	DRAND . . .	Chinese subjects, gilding.
	DUBOIS . . .	Flowers and garlands.
JD	DUROSEY, Julia .	Flowers, friezes, &c.
SD	DUROSEY, Soph. afterwards M[dme] NOUAILHER	Flowers, friezes, &c.
D	DUSOLLE . . .	Detached bouquets

Marks.	*Names of Painters.*	*Subjects.*
D T.	DUTANDA . . .	Bouquets, garlands.
	EVANS	Birds, butterflies, landscapes.
F	FALOT	Arabesques, birds, butterflies.
	FONTAINE . .	Emblems, miniatures.
	FONTELLIAU . .	Gilding.
Y	FOURÉ	Flowers, bouquets.
	FRITSCH . . .	Figures, children.
f z or f. x.	FUMEZ	Flowers, arabesques, &c.
	GAUTHIER . .	Landscapes, animals.
G	GENEST . . .	Figures, &c.
	GENIN	Figures, genre subjects.
G d.	GERRARD . . .	Pastorals, miniatures.
R...... or R	GIRARD . . .	Arabesques, Chinese subjects.
	GOMERY . . .	Birds.

Marks.	*Names of Painters.*	*Subjects.*
Gt.	GREMONT . .	Garlands, bouquets.
X or X.	GRISON . . .	Gilding.
Jh.	HENRION . .	Garlands, bouquets.
hc.	HERICOURT . .	Garlands, bouquets.
W or W	HILKEN . . .	Figures, subjects, &c.
H	HOUEY . . .	Flowers.
G or H.	HUNIJ . . .	Flowers.
J.	JOYAU . . .	Detached bouquets.
j.	JUBIN . . .	Gilding.
L or LR	LA ROCHE . .	Bouquets, medallions, emblems.
	LEANDRE . . .	Pastoral subjects.
Le.	LE BEL, Sen. .	Figures and flowers
LB or LB	LE BEL, Jun. .	Garlands, bouquets, insects.

Marks.	*Names of Painters.*	*Subjects.*
LF or *LF*	Unknown . .	Cupids, &c.
LL or LL	Lecot . . .	Chinese subjects.
◡	Ledoux . .	Landscapes and birds.
LG or LG	Le Guay . .	Gilding.
	Le Guay . .	Miniatures, children, trophies, Chinese.
L or L	Levé, père . .	Flowers, birds, and arabesques.
f	Levé, fils . .	Flowers, Chinese.
R.B	Maquerat, M dme, *née* Rachel Bouillat .	Flowers.
M	Massy . . .	Flowers and emblems.
ʃ or *S*	Mérault, Sen.	Various friezes.
9	Mérault, Jun.	Bouquets, garlands.
X	Michaud . .	Flowers, bouquets, medallions.
m or *M*	Michel . .	Detached bouquets.
M	Moiron . .	Flowers, bouquets.

Marks.	*Names of Painters.*	*Subjects.*
5.	MONGENOT .	Flowers, bouquets.
M or M	MORIN . . .	Marine and military subjects.
	MUTEL . . .	Landscapes.
n q	NIQUET. . .	Detached bouquets.
	NOEL . . .	Flowers, ornaments.
SD	NOUAILHER, M^{dme}, *née* Sophie DUROSEY . .	Flowers.
	PAJOU . . .	Figures.
P	PARPETTE, Philippe. .	Flowers.
L. P	PARPETTE, Louise . .	Flowers, garlands.
P.T.	PETIT . . .	Flowers.
f	PFEIFFER . .	Detached bouquets.
PH	PHILIPPINE the elder . . .	Children, genre subjects.
p.ª or p:	PIERRE, Sen. .	Flowers, bouquets.

Marks.	*Names of Painters.*	*Subjects.*
P7 or p7.	PIERRE, Jun. .	Bouquets, garlands.
S.j.	PITHOU, Sen. .	Portraits, historical subjects.
S.t	PITHOU, Jun. .	Figures, ornaments, flowers.
HP.	PREVOST . .	Gilding.
or	POUILLOT . .	Detached bouquets.
	RAUX . . .	Detached bouquets.
XX	ROCHER . . .	Figures.
	ROSSET . . .	Landscapes.
RL	ROUSSEL . . .	Detached bouquets.
S.h.	SCHRADRE . .	Birds, landscapes.
S S.p.	SINSSON, père .	Flowers.
or	SINSSON . . .	Flowers, groups, garlands.
	SIOUX . . .	Bouquets, garlands.
O	SIOUX, Jun. . .	Flowers and garlands, *en camaieu*.

Marks.	*Names of Painters.*	*Subjects.*
	TABARY . . .	Birds, &c.
	TAILLANDIER .	Bouquets, garlands.
• • •	TANDART . .	Bouquets, garlands.
	TARDI . . .	Bouquets, garlands.
• • • •	THEODORE . .	Gilding.
, or	THEVENET, Sen.	Flowers, medallions, groups.
jt.	THEVENET, Jun.	Ornaments, friezes.
VD	VANDÉ . . .	Gilding, flowers.
	VAUTRIN, afterwards Madame GERARD.	Bouquets, friezes.
W	VAVASSEUR . .	Arabesques, &c.
	VIELLARD . .	Emblems, ornaments
	VIELLARD . .	Emblems, ornaments
2000	VINCENT . . .	Gilding.
or	XHROUET . .	Arabesques, flowers
	YVERNEL . . .	Landscapes, birds.

MARKS OF PAINTERS (UNKNOWN).

J.F. ts VB

I.N. Am

Y B GI

LATE PERIOD, 1800 TO 1845.

Marks.	*Names of Painters.*	*Subjects.*
J. A.	ANDRE, Jules .	Landscapes.
AP	APOIL	Figures, subjects, &c.
E.AP.	APOIL, Mdme . .	Figures.
A.	ARCHELAIS . .	Ornaments.
P.A	AVISSE, Saul . .	Ornaments.
B	BARBIN, F. . .	Ornaments.
AB	BARRE	Flowers.
B.	BARRIAT . . .	Figures.

Marks.	*Names of Painters.*	*Subjects.*
B. r.	BERANGER . .	Figures.
B	BLANCHARD . .	Decorations.
A.B.	BLANCHARD, Alex. . . .	Ornaments.
B.T.	BOITEL	Gilding.
AB	BONNUIT . . .	Decorations.
AB	BOULLEMIER, A. .	Gilding.
F. B	BOULLEMIER, Sen.	Gilding.
Bf	BOULLEMIER, Jun.	Gilding.
Bx.	BUTEUX, Eug. .	Flowers.
JC	CABAU	Flowers.
C.P.	CAPRONNIER . .	Gilding.
I.G	CELOS	Decorations.
LC	CHARPENTIER .	Decorations.
F.C.	CHARRIN, Dlle Fanny . . .	Figures, subjects, portraits.
C.C.	CONSTANT . .	Gilding.

Marks.	*Names of Painters.*	*Subjects.*
C. T.	CONSTANTIN . .	Figures.
AD	DAMMOUSE . .	Figures and ornaments.
AD	DAVID, Alex.. .	Decorations.
D. F.	DAVIGNON . .	Landscapes.
D. F.	DELAFOSSE . .	Figures.
DC	DERICHSWEILER.	Decorations.
D P.	DESPERAIS . .	Ornaments.
Dh	DEUTSCH . . .	Ornaments.
C D	DEVELLY, C. . .	Landscapes and figures.
D. I.	DIDIER . . .	Ornaments.
D. T.	DROUET . . .	Flowers.
Ae. D.	DUCLUSEAU, M^{dme}	Figures, subjects, portraits.
Dy	DUROSEY . . .	Gilding.
HF	FARAGUET, M^{dme}.	Figures, subjects, &c.

Marks.	*Names of Painters.*	*Subjects.*
FC	FICQUENET . .	Flowers and ornaments.
F.	FONTAINE. . .	Flowers.
Th.F.	FRAGONARD . .	Figures, genre, &c.
Gu.	GANEAU, Jun. .	Gilding.
J.G.	GELY	Ornaments.
G:G.	GEORGET . . .	Figures, portraits.
Gob.R	GOBERT . . .	Figures in enamel on paste.
D.G.	GODIN	Gilding.
F.G.	GOUPIL . . .	Figures.
AG	GUILLEMAIN . .	Decorations.
H	HALLION, Eugène. . .	Landscapes.
H	HALLION, François	Gilding, decorations.
h.D.	HUARD . . .	Ornaments.
.E.H.	HUMBERT . .	Figures.

Marks.	*Names of Painters.*	*Subjects.*
JE	JULIENNE, Eug. .	Renaissance ornaments.
JL	LAMBERT . . .	Flowers.
L Gce.	LANGLACE . .	Landscapes.
LT	LATACHE . . .	Gilding.
L. B.	LE BEL . . .	Landscapes.
L.	LEGAY	Ornaments.
L. G.	LE GAY, Et. Ch.	Figures, portraits.
L. G.	LEGRAND . . .	Gilding.
EL	LEROY, Eugène .	Gilding.
M	MARTINET . .	Flowers.
E. de M	MAUSSION, Mlle de	Figures.
FM	MERIGOT, F. . .	Flowers and decorations.
	MEYER, Alfred .	Figures, &c.

Marks.	*Names of Painters.*	*Subjects.*
MC	MICAUD . . .	Gilding.
OM	MILET, Optat .	Decorations on fayence and paste.
MR	MOREAU . . .	Gilding.
AM	MORIOT . . .	Figures, &c.
P.P.	PARPETTE, D[lle] .	Flowers.
Ph.	PHILIPPINE . .	Flowers and ornaments.
P	PLINE	Gilding.
AP	POUPART, A.. .	Landscapes.
R or R.	REGNIER . . .	Figures, various subjects.
HR	REGNIER, Hyacinthe . . .	Figures, &c.
ER	REJOUX, Émile .	Decorations.
E 1,000	RENARD, Émile .	Decorations.
EMR	RICHARD, Émile	Flowers.

Marks.	*Names of Painters.*	*Subjects.*
E.R	RICHARD, Eugène	Flowers.
R	RICHARD, François	Decorations.
Jh.R.	RICHARD, Joseph	Decorations.
or	RICHARD, Paul .	Gilding.
R	RIOCREUX, Isidore	Landscapes.
Rx	RIOCREUX, Désiré-Denis . .	Flowers.
PR	ROBERT, Pierre .	Landscapes.
CR	ROBERT, Mdme .	Flowers and landscapes.
R	ROBERT, Jean François . .	Landscapes.
PMR	ROUSSEL . . .	Figures.
	SALON	Figures and ornaments.

Marks.	*Names of Painters.*	*Subiects.*
P.S.	SCHILT, Louis Pierre . . .	Flowers.
S.S.p	SINSSON, Pierre .	Flowers.
S.W.	SWEBACH . . .	Landscapes and figures.
J.T.	TRAGER, Jules .	Flowers, birds, ancient style.
T.	TROYON . . .	Ornaments.
W	WALTER . . .	Flowers.

POTTERY & PORCELAIN.

ENGLAND.

THOMAS TOFT
STAFFORDSHIRE, 1670.

RALPH TOFT 1677
STAFFORDSHIRE, 1670.

WILLIAM·SANS.
STAFFORDSHIRE, 1670.

WILLIAM·TALOR.
STAFFORDSHIRE, 1670.

RALPH TURNOR
1681.
STAFFORDSHIRE or WROTHAM.

IOSEPH.GLASS.S.Y.H.G.X
STAFFORDSHIRE, 1670.

WEDGWOOD.

Wedgwood.

WEDGWOOD
& BENTLEY.
BURSLEM, 1759. ETRURIA, 1769;
Bentley, 1768–80. W. died 1795.

Wedgwood
Wedgwood
Wedgwood
WEDGWOOD
WEDGWOOD
WEDGWOOD

JOSIAH WEDGWOOD
Feb 2 1805

WEDGWOOD
ETRURIA
WEDGWOOD
ETRURIA
Wedgwood
Etruria

WEDGWOOD
(*in red or blue*)

Emile Lessore
E Lessore
LB

ENGLAND

ELERS.
BRADWELL, 1690, ceased about 1700.

R. SHAWE.
BURSLEM, 1730 to 1740.

83
Ra. Wood
Burslem
BURSLEM, circa 1730 to 1750.

Aaron Wood
BURSLEM, 1750.

ENOCH WOOD.
BURSLEM, circa 1784.

THE REV^D
GEORGE WHITFIELD
died Sept 30. 1770
aged 56
ENOCH WOOD SCULP
BURSLEM

THE REV^D
JOHN WESLEY M.A.
died Mar 2. 1791
ENOCH WOOD SCULP
BURSLEM

WOOD and CALDWELL.

BURSLEM, 1790–1818, afterwards E. Wood and Sons.

E. WOOD & SONS.

STEEL.

BURSLEM, 1786; the works ceased 1824.

ALCOCK & CO.

BURSLEM. Established 1830.

BURSLEM.
Established about 1806, ceased 1839.

J. LOCKETT.

BURSLEM. Established about 1780.

Enoch Booth.

TUNSTALL. Established 1750.

A & E Keeling

TUNSTALL.
Succeeded Booth about 1770.

W. ADAMS.

TUNSTALL.
Established 1780; died 1804.

TUNSTALL. Recent; G. F. Bowers.

G. F. BOWERS

TUNSTALL

POTTERIES.

CHILD.

TUNSTALL. Smith Child, 1763.

ROGERS.

LONGPORT. Established about 1780.

ROGERS.

LONGPORT. Ceased 1829.

PHILLIPS,
LONGPORT.

LONGPORT. Established 1760.

LONGPORT.

Davenport
LONGPORT.

LONGPORT. John Davenport established 1793, and continued by his descendants to this day.

← 1887

R. DANIEL.

COBRIDGE. Established about 1710 and his son Ralph, 1743.

WARBURTON.

COBRIDGE or HOT LANE, 1710, continued by his widow.

COBRIDGE. Established circa 1814.

COBRIDGE. Established 1780, Stevenson and Dale, 1815 Stevenson alone.

VOYEZ.
1780.

J. VOYEZ

COBRIDGE. Established about 1773.

E. Mayer.

HANLEY. Established 1770, died 1813.

Joseph Meyer & Co., Hanley.

HANLEY.
Succeeded 1813, ceased 1830.

E. MEYER.

HANLEY.

MEIGH

HANLEY. Established 1780–1817; succeeded by his sons.

LAKIN & POOLE.

HANLEY.
Established 1770, ceased about 1800.

W. STEVENSON
HANLEY.
MAY.2.
1828.

Birch.

E.I.B.

HANLEY. Established last Century.

SHORTHOSE.

Shorthose.

Shorthose & Heath.

HANLEY. Established about 1770. Heath about 1800.

SALT.

HANLEY.
Established about 1815, died 1846.

MILES.

M 15

HANLEY. Established about 1700. his descendants about 1760.

HANLEY. Established 1760.

Neale & Palmer.

HANLEY.

HANLEY. Succeeded Palmer, 1776.

Neale & Co.

HANLEY, 1778.

Neale & Wilson.

HANLEY, 1778.

WILSON.

HANLEY.

C
WILSON

HANLEY. Robert about 1780, and his son David about 1800.

EASTWOOD

HANLEY.
W. Baddeley. Established about 1790, to 1820.

T. & J. HOLLINS.

HANLEY. Established 1780.

Keeling, Toft & Co.

HANLEY, 1806 to 1824. Succeeded by Toft and May, to 1830.

T. SNEYD
HANLEY.

HANLEY. End of last Century.

J. Keeling.

HANLEY. Succeeded Edward Keeling, 1802–1828.

HANLEY. Recent potters.

Mann & Co.
Hanley.

ASTBURY.

SHELTON. About 1710, died 1743.

S. HOLLINS.

SHELTON.
Established 1774, ceased 1816.

I. & G. RIDGWAY.
I. & W. RIDGWAY.

SHELTON. Bell Works. Established 1790, ceased 1854.

Ridgway & Sons.

SHELTON.
Cauldon Place. Established 1813.

SHELTON. Cauldon Place. J. and W. Ridgway, 1814–1830.

SHELTON. Cauldon Place. Circa 1830.

SHELTON.
Cauldon Place, 1850, ceased 1860.

SHELTON.
Cauldon Place. Established 1860.
Brown, Westhead, Moore & Co.

R. & J. BADDELEY.

SHELTON. Established 1750.

I. & E. BADDELEY.

SHELTON. Succeeded 1780–1806.

I. E. B.

SHELTON. *Ibid.*

HICKS, MEIGH & JOHNSON.

SHELTON. Succeeded 1806–1836.

R. M. W. & Co.

SHELTON. Succeeded 1836, Ridgway, Morley, Wear & Co.

Morley & Ashworth, Hanley.

SHELTON. Established by Whitehead, circa 1750. Taken by Champion's Company in 1782, ceased 1825.

HACKWOOD & CO.

SHELTON. Succeeded 1842.

C. & H. late HACKWOOD.

SHELTON. Cockson and Harding, succeeded, circa 1856.

YATES & MAY.

SHELTON.
Established by Yates, circa 1760.

MINTON.

MONOGRAM OF SOLON-MILES.

STOKE. Established 1790, by Thomas Minton, succeeded by Herbert M. in 1836, died 1858. Early mark.

Minton & Boyle, 1837.

MINTON'S.

M. & B.
Felspar China.

STOKE. Partner with Herbert, 1836.

STOKE. Minton's, used 1851.

STOKE. Minton
Used 1868.

(MINTON)

Each of the two brackets embracing the word "Minton" forming the letter C, and the mark therefore reading Colin Minton Campbell.

SPODE.

SPODE.
Felspar Porcelain.

STOKE. Established 1770, died 1797. Succeeded by his son Josiah.

SPODE, SON & COPELAND.

STOKE. W. Copeland, circa 1800.

Copeland, late Spode.

C. and G.

C and G.
New Blanche.

C and G.
Saxon Blue.

STOKE. Alderman W. T. Copeland purchased the Works, 1833. Copeland and Garrett, 1843.

STOKE. Alderman Copeland alone.

T. MAYER.

STOKE. Established about 1760. Succeeded by his son.

H. & R. DANIEL.

STOKE. Established about 1820, ceased in 1845.

WOLFE & HAMILTON. STOKE.

STOKE. Established 1776–1818. Hamilton joined, 1790.

WHIELDON.

FENTON.
Established 1740; died 1798. (Wedgwood in partnership until 1759.)

ELKIN KNIGHT & Co.

LANE DELPH now FENTON. About 1820.

FENTON STONE WORKS

FENTON.

MYATT

LANE DELPH. Established about 1780.

W. ADAMS.

STOKE. Died 1829, succeeded by

CLOSE & Co.

M. Mason.

MASON'S
CAMBRIAN ARGIL.

Mason's
Iron Stone China.

LANE DELPH. Established about 1780. Stone china patent, 1813. Succeeded by his son.

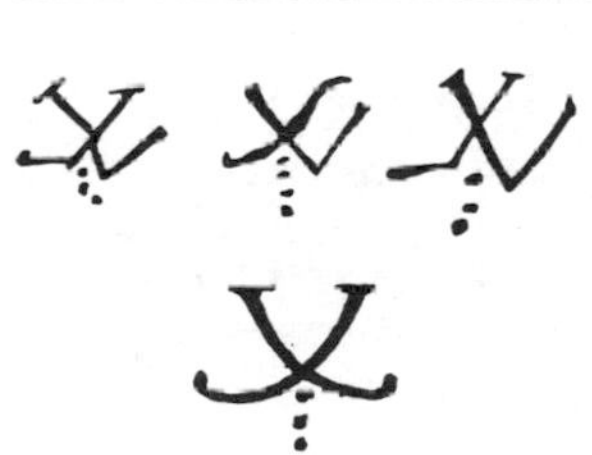

LONGTON HALL.

Aynsley.
Lane End.

LANE END. Established about 1780. Died 1826.

Bailey &Batkin.

LANE END. Established about 1800.

Mayr. & Newbd.
M & N.

LANE END.
Mayer & Newbold, about 1800.

T. Harley Laneend.

HARLEY.

LANE END. Established about 1790.

Cyples.
LANE END.

LANE END.
Hilditch and Son, about 1830.

LANE END.

B Plant
Lane End.

LANE END. Established about 1790.

TURNER.

LANE END. Banks and Turner in 1756; Turner alone, 1762; died 1786; succeeded by his sons.

Turner's Patent.

LANE END. William and John Turner's patent, 1820.

PEARL WARE.

LANE END.

CHETHAM & WOOLEY. PEARL WARE.

LANE END. Established about 1790.

T. GREEN. Fenton Pottery.

FENTON. Established about 1800.

ADAMS & PRINCE. Lane Delph.

Established about 1810.

W. BACCHUS. FENTON.

FENTON. Established about 1780.

Marshall & Co.

STAFFORDSHIRE.

G. Harrison.

STAFFORDSHIRE.

Uncertain Marks.

P & F W.

FREELING & Co.

C
I E
1748

T. H. & O.

Wilson & Proudman.

STAFFORDSHIRE. Uncertain.

LOWESBY, LEICESTERSHIRE.
Sir Francis Fowkes, 1835.

SHARPE,
MANUFACTURER,
SWADLINCOTE.

STAFFORDSHIRE. Uncertain.

Richard Chaffers
1769.

LIVERPOOL. Established 1752.
In 1756 he obtained Soap Rock from Cornwall; died 1767.

LIVERPOOL.

SHAW.

LIVERPOOL. Established about 1710.

SADLER
1756.

SADLER & GREEN.

LIVERPOOL. Inventors of transfer printing on china, 1756.

PENNINGTON.

P P

LIVERPOOL. Established 1760.

CHRISTIAN.

LIVERPOOL. Established 1760.

REID & Co.

LIVERPOOL.

LIVERPOOL.
Established 1790, by Richard Abbey, afterwards Worthington & Co.

HERCULANEUM
POTTERY.

HERCULANEUM.

LIVERPOOL. Ceased 1836.

W. Pierce and Co.

BENTHAL.

SALOPIAN
or
Salopian.

CAUGHLEY. Thos. Turner. Estabd. 1772. Willow pattern, 1780. Died 1799.

TURNER.

S

So S

CAUGHLEY. Turner, 1772–1799.

SALOPIAN.

CAUGHLEY. Turner, 1772–1799.

CAUGHLEY. Turner, 1772–1799.

C.D.

C Dale.

COLEBROOK DALE. Established 1785, by J. Rose, and XIX Century.

Coalport.

S

COALPORT. J. Rose. Established 1790; in 1820 he purchased Swansea and Nantgarw works.

MAW & CO.

BENTHAL.

WORCESTER.

W.P.C.

WORCESTER. Marks used before 1780.

July 31
1773

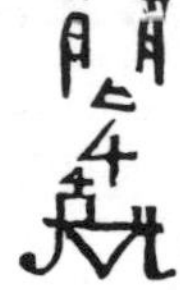

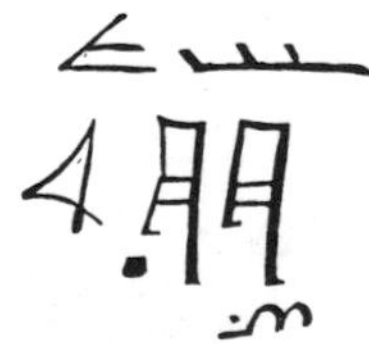

WORCESTER.
Marks used previous to 1780.

RH

Worcester.

WORCESTER.

RH Worcester

WORCESTER. Mark of Richard Holdship, about 1758, on transfer ware.

MONOGRAM OF JOHN DONALDSON, painter of Worcester China.

R Hancock fecit

WORCESTER.
R. Hancock, engraver, circa 1753.

C
Flight

Flight

Flight (crown above, crescent below)

B or **B** incuse

Barr Flight & Barr.

Flight Barr & Barr.

WORCESTER. Purchased by Flights in 1783; Barr joined in 1793.

Chamberlains

Chamberlain
Worcester

CHAMBERLAIN
WORCESTER.

WORCESTER. Established 1786; joined with Barr 1840.

MARKS USED ON WORCESTER PORCELAIN DURING THE "DOCTOR WALL" PERIOD, FROM 1751 TO 1783

(DR. WALL DIED IN 1776).

This complete list of Worcester marks during the best period of the factory includes several not given in any previous edition of Chaffers. The majority of them are taken, with Mr. Binns' courteous consent, from his Catalogue of the Collection of Worcester Porcelain in the Royal Porcelain Works Museum. Some of these are doubtless workmen's marks rather than trade or fabrique marks.

With reference to the Worcester marks below the following remarks may be added :—

Marks Nos. 1 to 56*a* are workmen's marks found on specimens of *printed* and *painted* blue decoration in the Museum of the Worcester Porcelain Works.

Marks Nos. 57 and 58—the open crescent—are, Mr. Binns says, the most usual mark on *painted* wares.

The filled-in crescent, No. 59, is only found on blue *printed* wares.

Marks are sometimes inconsistent with the decoration ; thus the cross swords will be found on a black transfer cup and saucer, and the square Chinese seal on a piece decorated in pattern anything but Oriental. This is on account of the blue fabrique mark having been put on before the piece was glazed or decorated.

Mark No. 64—the printed W—is very rare.

Marks No. 61, 70, 71, are all very scarce. The other marks are more usual, and excellent Worcester is frequently unmarked.

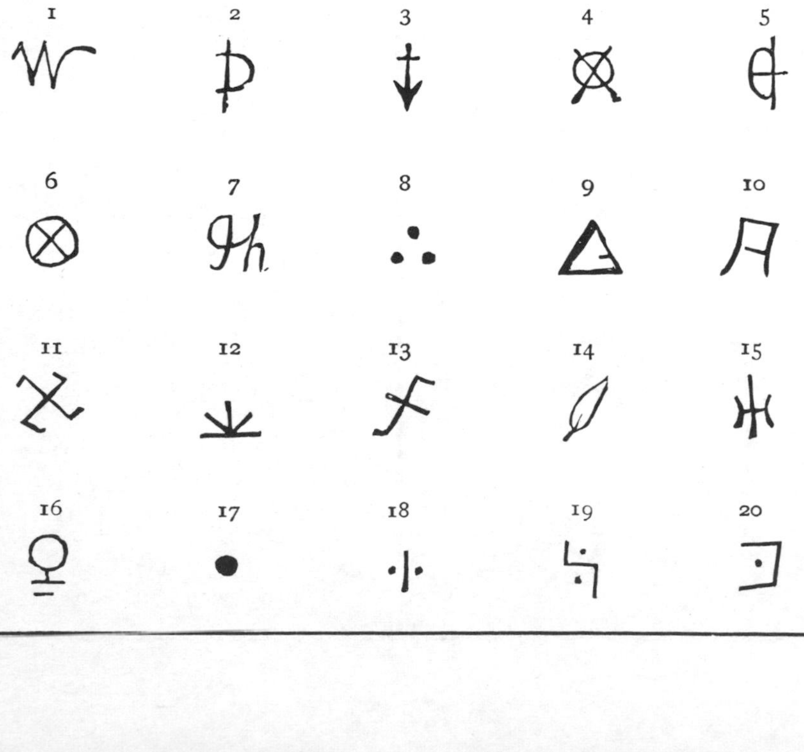

1 2 3 4 5

6 7 8 9 10

11 12 13 14 15

16 17 18 19 20

21 22 23 24 25

26 27 28 29 30

31 32 33 34 35

36 37 38 39 40

41 42 43 44 45

46 47 48 49 50

51 52 53 54 55

55*a* 56 56*a* 57 58

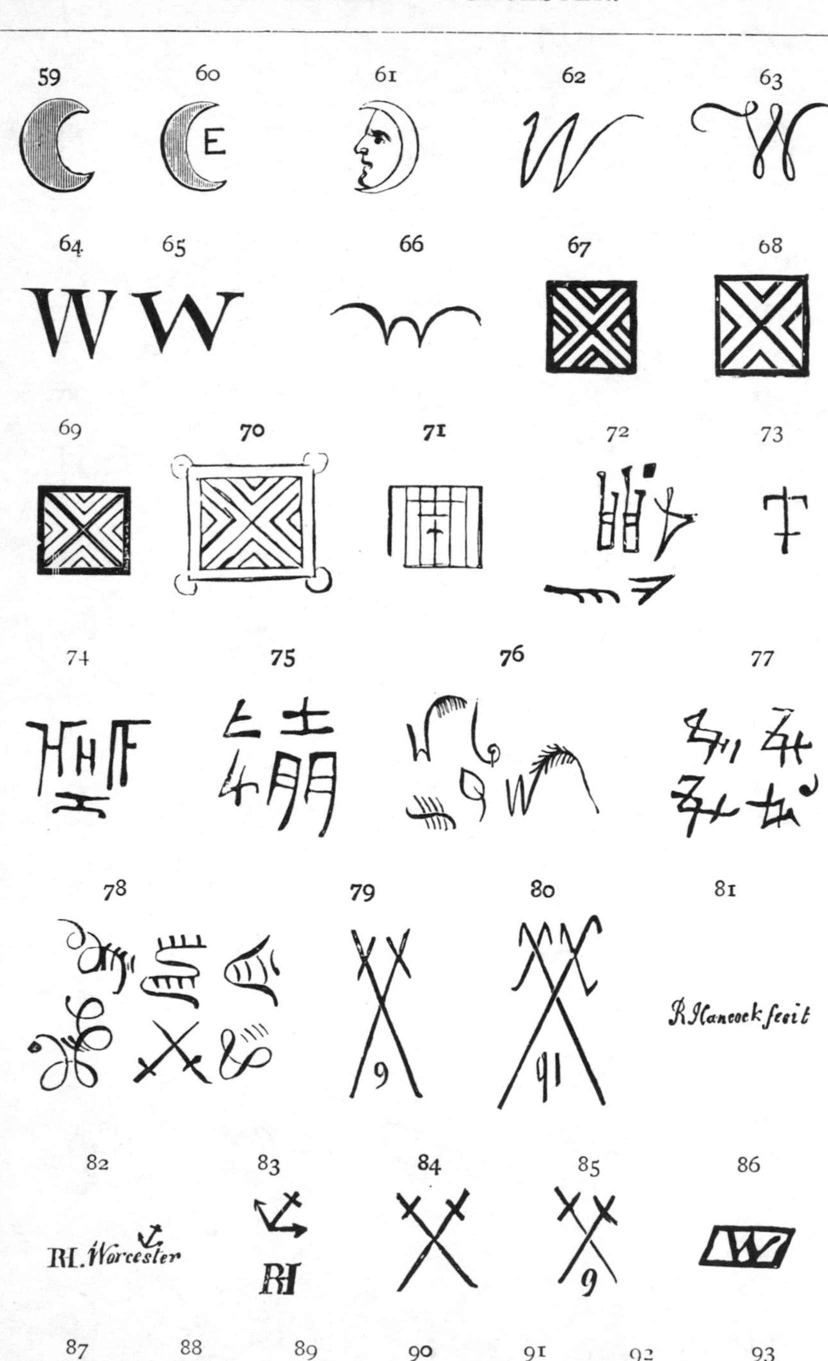
59
60
E
61
62
63
64
65
66
67
68
69
70
71
72
73
74
75
76
77
78
79
9
80
91
81
R Hancock fecit
82
RI. Worcester
83
RH
84
85
9
86
W
87
88
89
90
91
92
93
94
95
96
97
98
99

WORCESTER.
Messrs. Kerr & Binns, 1852 to 1862.

WORCESTER. Messrs. Kerr & Binns.
Present mark since 1862.

WORCESTER PORCELAIN COMPANY (LIMITED).
Established 1862.

Grainger Lee and Co.
WORCESTER.

WORCESTER. Established 1800.

George Grainger
Royal China Works
Worcester.

WORCESTER. Geo. Grainger succeeded his father, 1839.

Leeds Pottery

LEEDS.
Established 1760, by Messrs. Green.

Hartley, Greens & Co.
LEEDS POTTERY.

LEEDS. Partners, 1783.

GREEN.
LEEDS.

C G
W

LEEDS POTTERY
LEEDS POTTERY

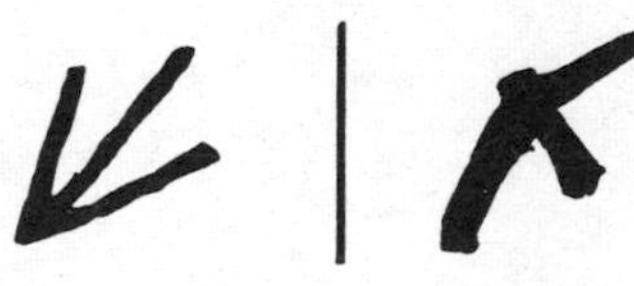

C G

LEEDS. Other marks.

D. D. & Co.
CASTLEFORD
POTTERY.

CASTLEFORD. Established 1790, by D. Dunderdale; ceased 1820.

DON POTTERY.

GREEN.
DON POTTERY.

DONCASTER. Established 1790, by J. Green, in 1807 Clark joined.

HULL. Established about 1820, by Mr. W. Bell.

MIDDLESBRO
POTTERY CO.

MIDDLESBORO', about 1820 to 1850.

FERRYBRIDGE.

WEDGWOOD & Co.

FERRYBRIDGE. Established 1792, by Tomlinson and others; joined by Ralph Wedgwood in 1796.

1712 ATIC

YEARSLEY. Wedgwood, 1700.

REED.

MEXBOROUGH. Established about 1800. Beevers and Co. Mr. Reed, 1839.

ROCKINGHAM.

Rockingham Works.
Brameld.

Brameld.

SWINTON, called ROCKINGHAM. Established 1757, by T. Butler, &c. In 1807, Bramelds. Ceased 1842.

DIXON, AUSTIN, & Co.

DIXON & Co.
Sunderland Pottery.

SUNDERLAND. Established about 1810.

Scott, Brothers & Co.

SUNDERLAND. Established 1788.

PHILLIPS & Co.
Sunderland 1813.

PHILLIPS & Co.
Sunderland Pottery.

SUNDERLAND. Established about 1800.

J. PHILLIPS,
Hylton Pottery.

SUNDERLAND. Established about 1780.

SUNDERLAND.

DAWSON.

SUNDERLAND. Established about 1810.

FELL.

T. FELL & Co.

NEWCASTLE-UPON-TYNE.
Established 1800.

Sheriff Hill Pottery.

NEWCASTLE. Established by Mr. Lewins, about 1800.

SEWELL
ST. ANTHONY'S.

SEWELL & DONKIN.

NEWCASTLE. Established 1780.

MOORE & CO.
SOUTHWICK.

SUNDERLAND. Established 1789, by Brunton and Co.

STOCKTON
POTTERY.

W. S. & Co.
QUEENS. WARE.
STOCKTON.

STOCKTON. Established about 1810, by W. Smith and J. Whalley.

John Smith Junr of Basford near Nottingham. 1712.

NOTTINGHAM.
Established 1700. In 1751, Morley, maker of brown stoneware.

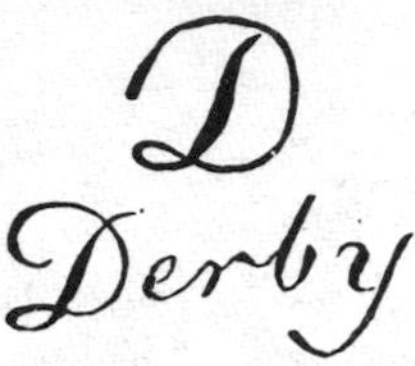

DERBY.
Established 1751, by W. Duesbury.
Early marks.

DERBY.

E
1779

CHELSEA-DERBY. Used 1769 to 1780.

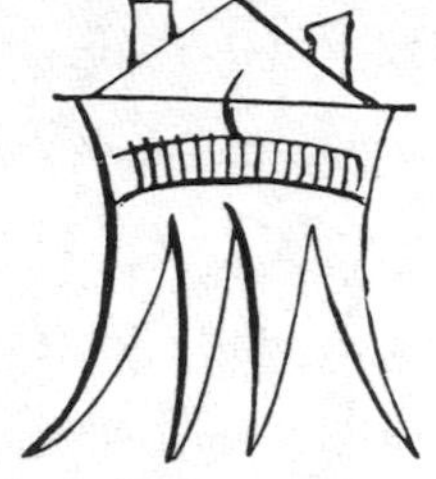

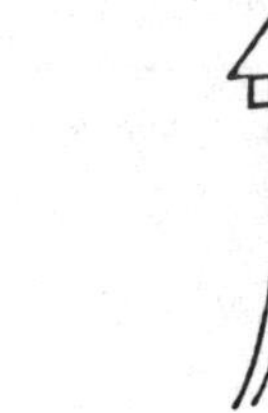

CHELSEA-DERBY. Before 1780.

CROWN DERBY.
Used 1780. Duesbury and Kean.

W. DUESBURY.
1803.

CROWN DERBY.
Marks used from 1780 to 1815.

DERBY. Richard Holdship. On transfer printed ware.

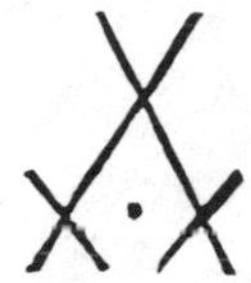

DERBY. Early mark.

Bloor. Succeeded 1815—to 1839.

Locker. Succeeded 1849.

DERBY. Courtney was Bloor's London agent.

DERBY. Stevenson and Co. in 1859.

DERBY. Stevenson and Hancock, 1859.

DERBY. Modern.

Allen
Lowestoft

LOWESTOFT.

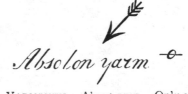

Absolon yarm

YARMOUTH. About 1790. Only a decorator, not a manufacturer.

I E 1707
WROTHAM

WROTHAM, KENT. 1656–1710.

PAYNE,
SARUM.

SALISBURY. A Dealer.

March
14
1768
C F

Cookworthy's Factory.

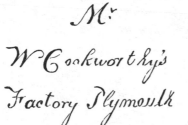

W Cookworthy's
Factory Plymouth
.1770.

PLYMOUTH. Established 1768, by Cookworthy. Ceased 1772.

24

PLYMOUTH MARKS, 1768–1772.

B 7

BRISTOL.

Bristoll.

BRISTOL.

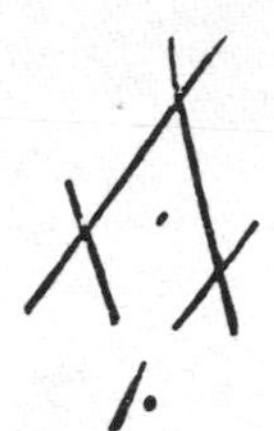

T°

BRISTOL.
Established 1770, by Champion, who purchased Cookworthy's patent in 1772. Ceased 1777.

BRISTOL POTTERY. Established 1777. Ring and Co.

Robert Asslet,
17 *London Street* 21

FULHAM STONEWARE.

FULHAM. W. de Morgan.

Wm GOULDING
June 20th 1770.

ISLEWORTH. Established 1760, by Shore; ceased 1800.

LAMBETH—DOULTON'S FAYENCE AND STONEWARE.

DOULTON
IMPASTO

DOULTON
& SLATER'S
PATENT

DOULTON'S FAYENCE—ARTISTS' SIGNATURES.

Miss HANNAH B. BARLOW.

Mr. ARTHUR B. BARLOW.

Mr. GEORGE TINWORTH.

Miss COLLINS.

Miss F. LINNELL.

Miss M. CAPES.

Miss Crawley.

Miss F. Lewis.

Mr. John Eyre.

Miss Kate Rogers.

RK

Miss Rosa Keen.

MB or

Miss Mary Butterton.

Miss Edwards.

Miss Florence Barlow.

Mr. Butler.

M·V·M

Mr. Mark Marshall.

MARTIN'S SOUTHALL STONEWARE.

10, 1896

Martin Bros
London & Southall

9, 1896

R. W. Martin & Bros
London & Southall

10, 1897

Martin Brothers
London & Southall

These marks are scratched in cursive autographs.

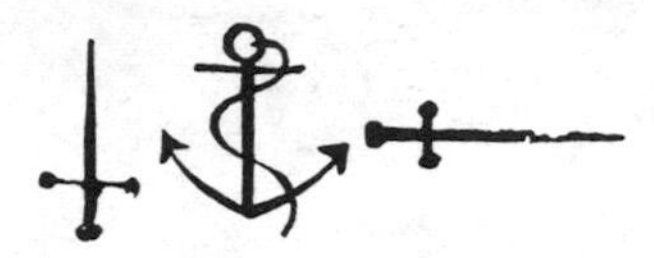

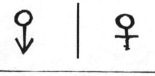

Bow. Established 1730; ceased 1775. Transferred to Derby.

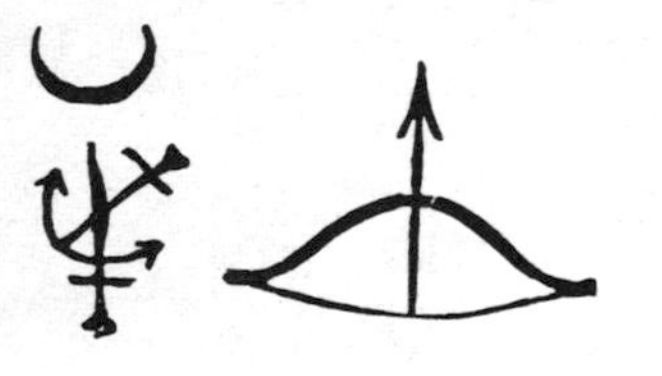

Bow Marks, 1730–1775.

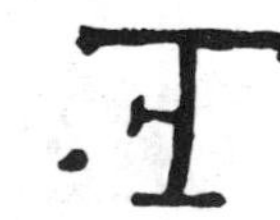

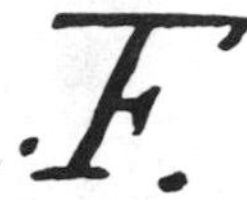

Bow Marks.

Bow. Monograms of Thomas Frye.

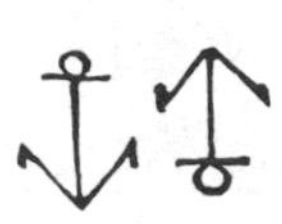

Chelsea. Established 1745; ceased 1769. Transferred to Duesbury, of Derby.

Chelsea. Incised mark (very early).

Cambrian Pottery

CAMBRIAN

HAYNES, DILLWYN & Co.
CAMBRIAN POTTERY,
SWANSEA.

Swansea. Established 1750; taken by G. Haynes, 1780; ceased 1820, and removed to Coalport.

OPAQUE CHINA.

SWANSEA.

Swansea.

SWANSEA

DILLWYN & Co

SWANSEA

SWANSEA. Marks.

M.W. & Co

LLANELLY. Founded by Chambers. In 1868, Worenzou and Co.

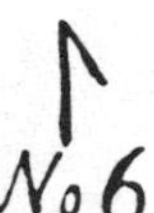

No 6

NANTGARW. Established 1813, by Billingsley; ceased 1820.

NANTGARW.

Dublin

DUBLIN. Uncertain. About 1760.

DONOVAN.

Donovan,
Dublin.

DUBLIN, 1790.
Donovan, a decorator only.

BELLEEK. Established 1856, by Messrs. Armstrong and McBirney.